Aspects Of
Love

A Collection Of Poetry
Edited by Donna Samworth

First published in Great Britain in 2012 by:
Forward Poetry
Remus House
Coltsfoot Drive
Peterborough
PE2 9BF
Telephone: 01733 890099
Website: www.forwardpoetry.co.uk

All Rights Reserved
Book Design by Ashley Janson
© Copyright Contributors 2012
SB ISBN 978-1-84418-601-3

Foreword

Here at Forward Poetry our aim has always been to provide a bridge to publication for unknown poets and allow their work to reach a wider audience. We believe that poetry should not be exclusive or elitist but available to be accessed and appreciated by all.

For our latest anthology we invited writers to submit a poem on the theme of love. The result is a fantastic and varied collection of verse about love in all its forms, whether everlasting love, family love, unrequited love or even love for chocolate. Whether you prefer humourous rhymes or poignant odes there is something inside these pages that will suit every reader's taste.

We are very proud to present this anthology and we are sure it will provide entertainment and inspiration for years to come.

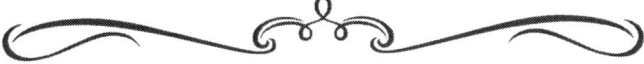

Contents

Josephine Rogers	1
Mary Stubbs	2
John Matthews	2
Lindy Roberts	3
Muireen Dunn	4
Jessica Stephanie Powell	5
Barbara C Perkins	6
Caroline Ferguson	7
Audrey Moore	7
Susan Biggin	8
Nancy Sarro	8
Timothy Gutteridge	9
Barry Bradshaigh	9
Heather Clark	10
Kevin Grieveson	10
Terry-Anne James-Davies	11
Andy MacDonald	11
Andy Fawthrop	12
Marie Black	13
Stacey Busuttil	14
Jessica Williamson	15
David Richards	16
Monica Partridge	16
Kathy Carr	17
Edna Sparkes	17
Craig Bumpus	18
Kyle Winstone-Evans	18
John Howe	19
Sharon Waring	19
Thomas Hudson	20
Nikita Liebscher	21
Robert John Ponting	22
Sullivan The Poet	23
Michael McArdle	23
Ian Lumley	24
Eve M Turner	25
Robert Stevens	26
Joyce Chaffer	26
Stephen P B West	27
Emma-Louise Gardner	27
Cecilia Neil-Smith	28
Marie Erskine	28
Daniel Winter	29
David Holmes	29
Jane Baker	30
Ben Corde	31
Ann Parkinson	32
Amanda Thompson	34
Moira Whittley	35
Barbara Leswell	35
Philip Boote	36
Jim Spain	37
Fiona Pearse	38
Derek Dobson	38
Len A Hynds	39
Nicola Brooks-Williamson	39
Vera Tyrer Collins	40
Katie Elizabeth Howell	41
Linda Casey	42
Tom Brealey	42
Julianne Clarke	43
Nigel Pearce	43
Denis Martindale	44
Ernest-Wilhelm Peters	45
Charlotte Crisp	45
Hannah Dickinson	46
Michael Bracken	47
Nicolas Bowyer	48
Tony Ellis	48
Catherine Butterfield	49
Lauren Brazier	49
Dr Nithie Victor	50
Stephanie Edwards	51
Bill Fletcher	51
Ernest Roberts	52
Dee Makanda	52
Frank Pavitt	53
Sharon Boothroyd	54
Rosalind J Lee	55
Elizabeth Morton	56
Farzana Nadeem	56
James Stephen Cameron	57
Keith Newing	57
Kevin Crookes	58
Charlotte Barnes	58
Fred Brown	59
Stephen Mortlock	60
Jackie Hinden	60
Jade Smith	61
Doreen Carne	61
Kathy Patton McLemore	62
George R Bell	62

Name	Page		Name	Page
Robert Newton	63		Saara Mahomed	96
Tony Newman	63		Hayley Rowe	96
Lucy Edwards (15)	64		Von Corner	97
Denise Jarrett	65		Sophie Revell	98
Matthew Fitzsimmons	66		Ramandeep Kaur	100
Lynn Widdows	66		Sherrie Molyneaux	101
Samuel Saleem Fisher	67		Janet Vessey	102
William Weavings	67		David Cameron	103
Tiffany Aubrey	68		Mike Whaley	103
Doina Postolachi	69		Ezekiel Headley	104
Susan Mullinger	69		Nassira Ouadi	105
Nasima Begum	70		Steffi McIntyre	106
Kumbi Johnson	70		Stephen Smith	106
Natalia Gorodova	71		Sandra McGowan	107
Thandiwe Tafireyi	71		Eva Kaye	107
Julie Gibbon	72		Josephine Smith	108
Eilidh Fergusson	72		Fine Buliciri	109
Frances Robson	73		Lianne Lee	110
Sara Baker	73		Patrick Jefferies	111
David M Walford	74		Elizabeth Fleischer	111
Rujina Akther	75		Michele Amos	112
Lynda Johns	76		Kelly Louise Meacock	112
Ghazal Choudhary	78		James Tracey-Burner	113
Ryan Manning	78		Anna Hands	113
Michael Robertson	79		Kieran Davis	114
Lee Hunt	80		Dat Guy Dere	115
Peter Davies	81		Amy Hughes	115
Gillian Fisher	81		Stacey Hubbard	116
Suzanne Stevenson	82		Rebecca Taunton	117
Rasharda Thompson	82		Unbreen Shabnum Aziz	117
Oxana Poberejnaia	83		Lorraine Hayley Mosley Coburn	118
Carena Mills	83		Aaron Noel	119
Muhammad Khurram Salim	84		Jon Cooper	119
Dale Alun Duggan	84		Peter Payne	120
Carolyn Fittall	85		Adam Leese	120
Sarah George	85		Nikolai Holding	121
Aleksandra Petrova	86		Hannah O'Brien	122
Prof Mary May Robertson	87		Glynnis Morgan	123
Piotr Gabryelski	88		Ethan Chapples	124
Tony Kangah	88		Tabitha Lay	124
Adwoa Asiedu	89		Aqeel Ali	125
Saba Ikhlas Malik	90		Swapna Haddow	125
Ellis Elliott	90		Harry Hunt	126
Demetra Ciobanu	91		Stacey Reay	127
Charles Baylis	91		Dan Long	128
Carmina Masoliver	92		John Stewart	129
Stephen Foot	92		Nandita Keshavan	129
Lisa Jane Mills	93		Nadia Bennett	130
Barbara R Lockwood	94		Joseph Hankinson	131
Ron Constant	95		Mary Webb	132

Name	Page
Douglas Drummond	132
Rev Ralph A Watkins	133
Beverly Maiden	133
Martin Selwood	134
Paula Holdstock	134
James Thompson	135
Paul M Clarkson	136
Barry Scott Crisp	137
James Howden	138
Adrian Bullard	139
Paula Greene	139
Tom O'Mara	140
Rev Prof John Beazley	140
Anthony David Beardsley	141
John Bliven Morin	141
Dori Wheeler	142
Will Martin	143
Thomas McDougall	143
Bill Hayles	144
Robin Martin-Oliver	145
Rachel Hughes	145
Adrian G McRobb	146
Carly Burns	146
Terry John Powell	147
Michael Forester	148
Jennifer Louise Hudson	149
Darren James Lee	150
Changjiang Zhang	152
Graham Hayden	152
Ian Cresswell	153
Peter Madden	154
Jeanette Gaffney	155
Elaine Catherine Christie	155
Donna Giblin	156
William Forsyth	156
Sam Sebbage	157
Starchild Moondust	158
Mark Mikkelsen	159
Bernard Harry Reay	160
Neil Douglas Tucker	161
Charlotte Murray	162
Gavin Cooke	162
Stephanie Caldwell	163
Sue Meredith	163
Roy Hare	164
Elizabeth Corr	164
Huw Parsons	165
Angela Wells	166
Tatenda Mushayi	167
Jonathan Simms	167
Mary Woolvin	168
Janet Starkey	169
Warren Kemp	170
Tracy Allott	171
Charlotte O'Farrell	172
William Green	173
Paul Kelly	173
Hassan Imran	174
Tim Kitchen	175
Natalie Williams	176
Carole Dickinson	176
Elizabeth Green	177
Heather Harwood	177
Cedric A Thrupp	178
Emma McNamara	178
Rachel Van Den Bergen	179
Robert Black	179
Kayt Pritchard	180
Ann Warren	180
Margaret Pace	181
Caroline Jones	182
Peter Mahoney	183
Natalie Moores	184
John Waby	185
Ann Barefoot	186
Shirley Johnson	186
Meia Alegranza	187
Mick Nash	188
Rita Mateus	190
Jagdeesh Sokhal	190
Allan Brebner	191
Patricia J Tausz	192
David M Walford	192
Chris Watts	193
David Chrzanowski	193
Andrew Fisher	194
Serita Blake	194
Jackie Joseph	195
Yazmin White	195
Lisa Burton	196
Frances M Searle	197
Teresa Webster	198
Cathy Mearman	198
Harry Stevenson	199
Laura Muskin	199
Mary Pauline Winter, nee Coleman	200
Mike Silkstone	201
Nicola Jean Holden	202
Steve Waterfield	202
Jim Ryder	203

Joseph Fairhurst 203	Minerva Pinciu 241
Michael Green 204	Roman Mikhalyuk 242
Nadia Fahmy 205	Anne Senanayake 242
Deborah Storey 205	Igor Marinovsky 243
Sigrid Marceau 206	Michael Kwaku Kesse Somuah 243
M Groves 206	Kagiso Basetsana Makwatse 244
Susie Sullivan 207	Pushkar Bisht 245
Nadine Smart 207	Lisa La Grange 245
Gillian Saunders 208	Sarah Zhu 246
Jill Truman 208	Rev Gideon Sampson Cecil 247
Sheila Sharpe 209	Jerome Teelucksingh 248
Sue Gerrard 210	Michael Seese 249
Liam Ó Comáin 211	Carla Iacovetti 249
Jigna Patel 211	Umesh Rao 250
Chris Glover 212	Zinzile Mngomezulu 251
Nathan Rowark 213	Shirley Harrison 251
David Russell 214	Nan Collain 252
Bill Eden 215	Adrian Pickett 253
Gordon Bruce 215	Nikita Biswal 254
Liz Davies 216	Mukesh Williams 255
Peter Thomas 217	Dinah van der Werf 256
Billie Dee Gianfrancesco 218	Anila Pillai 257
Kenneth Mood 219	Zoha Khalid 258
Marc Carver 220	Tersia De Jager 259
Natalie Rogers 221	Mukeshkumar Raval 260
Leigh Jones 222	
John Greeves 222	
Peter Steele 223	
Barry Pankhurst 223	
Colin Burnell 224	
David Youlden 225	
Steven Michael Pape 226	
Sally Plumb 226	
Robin Lindsay Wilson 227	
Antoinette Marshall 228	
Gwendoline Douglas 229	
Nick Clifton 230	
June Smith 231	
Betty Lightfoot 232	
Jonathan Bryant 233	
Pauline Hamilton 234	
Grace Maycock 235	
Kevin Ryan 236	
Leonard A G Butler 237	
Susan Jacqueline Roberts 237	
Ray Ryan 238	
Janet Harmer 239	
Laraine Smith 240	
Michael Levy 241	

The Poems

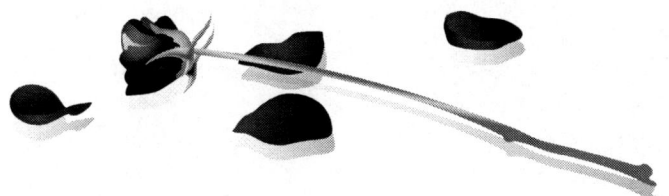

ASPECTS OF *Love* - A Collection Of Poetry

On Her Way To Hampstead

The wind pulls at her skirt
As she stands waiting for the four-thirty-six to Hampstead,
Squinting in the cold.
The industrial wind ravages her brown hair billowing,
Her coat, shades of blue,
Her cheeks a rosy ice-pink hew.
You wish to be the breeze which tickles her neck,
The skin her scarf cannot hide from the freeze.
The train pulls up tauntingly
And the moments she is obscured by the machinery-beast.
You crane your neck with falling subtlety,
Just to see her one last time, at least.
The train doors snap shut sharply,
And you catch a giddy glimpse of that famous face
Through the dirty breath-stained windows.
She takes a seat, and takes a glance outside,
Her eyes drift across scurrying robot-people,
Past clumps of hats and shifting duffle coats,
And rest slowly upon your face, still and chillingly beautiful.
From across the tracks and graffiti marks,
She smiles through eyes like seas of sharks,
Skies of storms
And dreams unborn.
Travelling with gathering speed,
Your wish she cannot heed,
She does not know you,
She will forget your head,
And the words you never said,
On her way to Hampstead.

Josephine Rogers

Well Done Josephine!

your poem has won you £25!

UNTITLED

She stands alone with eyes abrim
With tears,
Seeing ahead the empty years,
No one sees inside your broken heart,
Or how her life is torn apart,
At the sight of the empty chair,
How can life be so unfair,
She longs to feel his gentle touch,
Sometimes she feels it's all too much
The everlasting yearning
That is in her heart still burning,
She stands alone
Recalling all the love and all the laughter,
Hoping to share it all again in
God's holy hereafter.

Mary Stubbs

UNTITLED

Love is silver, pure and believing
Love is mercury, quick and deceiving
Love is gold, beauty revealing
Love is a diamond, brilliant and enduring
Love is you, soft and appealing
Love is me, strong and still needing
Love is all life
Love is all
Love is
Love.

John Matthews

WITHOUT LOVE

To love and be loved is the only one happiness
Without love in our lives it can seem pointless
We all need love, to love, when loved we are blessed.

Without love we will always be so very lonely,
And we will not grow to the person we wish to be
When we are not loved our lives will seem empty.

Most of us crave to be loved, it's something we all long
Without love we can sink into anxiety and depression
Love offers you more joy than anything material or possession.

And without love there will always be a hunger
When we are loved we are all happier and healthier
By loving each other we grow younger, live longer.

We all need to be loved, without it we wither and die
Like air, water, food, it's an ingredient we need to survive
Love is really absolutely vital for all human life.

When someone loves us it can make our heart sing
And love is the magic potion that will give us wings
Love can make us feel secure, safe, it's so healing.

Everybody in the world wants love, each and everyone
When loved you are like a teenager, and feel young
Being in love gives you so much joy, it's lots of fun.

Love is the only magic that can put things right
And it is the one most important thing in our life
It can turn our dark world into the brightest light.

And love raises you to heights that seem impossible
It is a true miracle, the strongest, the most powerful
Without love then you will have nothing at all . . .

Lindy Roberts

Rest In These Arms

Rest in these arms
Rest for a while
No sighing, no crying
Oh sweet love of mine

I know of your suffering
I know of your pain
I will move Heaven and Earth
My love will remain

I am here for you only
I am here till the end
The love we had will never end

I will catch your dreams
I will watch you sleep
I will watch over you
Slumbering deep

My love will surround you
Miracles to astound you
My faith will heal you
Angels will be near you
My prayers will be answered to you
My voice will sing to you
My strength will be you
My light will shine on you
Forever beside you
My arms will reach out to you
My ears will listen to you
My lips will blow kisses to you
My feet will walk in your way
Every second of every day
My soul shall keep you warm
From the cold and bitter storms
This I give to you
Thee only love I ever knew.

Muireen Dunn

DO YOU REMEMBER ME?
(This poem is dedicated to all that are affected by Alzheimer's, Dementia, and other memory loss related illnesses)

Do you remember me?
Or are you lost to me forever?
Do you remember that summer we had so much fun?
The children running around.
Splashing in the sea.
On your shoulder they would take turns
Being carried.
Ice cream in hand
Castles built on the sand.
Hand in hand
Off we went exploring the world.
Without a care in the world.
You and me didn't have
In a happy bubble we lived
Ignorant of what would shatter our blissful existence.
We used to stroll along the sandy beach
As the sea came back and forth across the bare feet.
How I would give anything for us to be back there.
Not here watching you sailing away from this life
into another world far from us.
If I kissed you, would you know me?
Or would you look up with
searching eyes trying to remember anything . . .
But it's no good.
We have grandchildren now but . . .
Tomorrow your thoughts will not be any clearer though.
I have happy memories, and the children, family and friends too
They keep me going through the dark days.
But who do you have now the illness has set in?
Are you scared, frightened?
Me too.
What now my love?
Is this goodbye forever?
Do you remember us?
Or are you lost to us forever?

Jessica Stephanie Powell

TO LOVE

I just want
To feel it
Just once before I die
Subtle tones
Of purity
Sensual, pleasure, high

To feel the
Warmth of human flesh
Against my body, pressed
To explore the
Endless boundaries
From my hips to breast

To feel
Contorting
Muscles, bone and sweat
To lose all
Sense of being
Float away, forget

Breathless
In the moment
Feelings, magnified
Sensitivity
Heightened
The mood intensified

To feel the rush
Of fire
Burning in my blood
To taste you
And to savour it,
The essence of true love

I just want
To feel it
Just once before I die
Harmonious,
Contentment
Bound together, tied.

Barbara C Perkins

UNENDING LOVE

Unending love is a love that's pure and true
From a mother to her child
A love that I once knew

Adoring eyes with lips that always smile

How sweet it is to be loved when you're a child
To share her thoughts, her life and all she can

For her sweet little lady
Or her cute little man

To be a part of a family like this

A gentle hug or a mother's loving kiss
To be taught life's ways at your mother's knee.

No better way your little life can be.
What a joy for a child to see

How a happy family should be
And as we grow we learn to love in return

Our little ones will not be concerned
Their lives will be happy for sure

Now we have grown and we are so secure
Unending love is all we ever need to grow and
In life to succeed.

Caroline Ferguson

LOVE . . . LOST AND FOUND

We sat side by side in the Old School field, and he made me daisy chains;
We argued and fought and often fell out, but we loved making up again!
We tramped for miles with the wind in our hair, and laughed in the sun or the rain . . .
Then fate intervened and changed our lives, and I'll never forget that pain.
But now and again I see him around, and both of us wave and smile,
And the memories all come flooding back, of the love we shared for a while.
Then I turn away, and standing there, through a mist of nostalgic tears
I see the one who loves me now . . . and will through the coming years

Audrey Moore

A Death In Venice – Non Ti Ho Amato Mai Tanto

Enamoured, Italia, still I care,
Let me love longer and keep you near,
Sustain my ocean-deep affair.
Soft Lido waters, drink my tears:
For the winds have changed, I must – prepare,
To – leave; but a final carefree dream
On waves of Petrach's hills afloat
Concede me, comforted, lapped to sleep.
Ah, Circe charms – I can't let go
With Monteverdi in my ears.

Perhaps I yet could find a way,
Excogitate a compromise,
To keep those views of Naples Bay,
To smell the Carso's resined pines;
To call out Raphael by name,
To muse how Giotto drew his 'O',
To bask in Dante's mystery,
To study Fra Angelico . . .
I have it! Let me keep a key,
So always I can claim you mine.

Susan Biggin

My World

In my world you mean so much,
I long for your tender touch
The way you shy away
Makes me want to be with you every day.

Days without you seem so long and the nights so far beyond
Wildest ever dreams of you keep me living
And you too.

Your dreams of life and the world around.
I could listen to you forever because I love what I've found.
So keep on dreaming one day they might come true,
One day in my world it will be just me and you.

Nancy Sarro

Forgive The Ways

Forgive the way I treated you
Tormenting you each day
Forgive the way I never found
The perfect words to say
Forgive the way I stood and watched
As your heart was wrenched in two
Forgive the way I caused you hurt
The pain I shared with you.
Forgive the way I never stood
And held you in my arms
Forgive the way I left you there
Abandoning your charms
Forgive the way I cannot move
To pastures with more hope
Forgive the way I am a fool
And wouldn't let you cope
If you cannot forgive the ways
Remember only this
I forgive you, in every way
Live in peace and bliss.

Timothy Gutteridge

Et Philos

Between two heartbeats moments butterfly,
Emotions tingles, breath awaits in grasp,
To zing desire in quivers thrilling hie,
And climax longs in kisses throbbing gasp.
Then shall the love we bare unite in w-rest,
Of ruby lips in sweetest love concur,
So succulent to sun so fresh and blest,
That ripe is joy and ecstasy its fleur.
Then in hearts kitchen heat of loves concord,
Eyes egg the beat that cakes in Leah's hope,
And whips in sweeps cloth plays of nips discord,
As smiled cheese toasts so hot as lovers grope.
Then chilly be not hot but love amore,
Or chilli be not heat but hearts adore.

Barry Bradshaigh

A Human Blessing

It involves pain and tears,
Associates with fear of death,
Complicates life and destroys happiness.

Avoid it at all costs,
It casts an irreversible curse,
And ties two together for eternity.

It provokes absurd beliefs,
Causes some to act selflessly,
Creates prisoners from heroes.

Fight this villain now,
Before it gets you too,
Don't be fooled by its cover.

Could you honestly spend a life,
Dreaming only one dream,
Hearing only one song?

That is what it will do,
It has no advantages,
It is love.

Heather Clark

Where Is The Love

There is a love for all of your family
Like Mother, Father, Sister, Brother
Daughter and Son.

But where is the love for you?
It is like a strange hold or
A kick in the teeth
That becomes no pleasure and cannot get away.

So the love you crave for can become
Like a second, a minute, an hour, a day
Or a lifetime of searching.

Kevin Grieveson

Doggy Love Song

Love is a dog's bottom,
There to be sniffed with joy,
Finding a new friend in the park.
A dog's bottom is his
Carefully crafted
Love poem
Sending out all the right signals;
Airborne, charged with electricity
And attraction,
Tail wagging,
Waiting and hoping to be loved.

Terry-Anne James-Davies

Last Night

My world came crashing down round my ears last night
Asked her out for a few beers last night
Took the bus 'cause a taxi was too dear last night
She played our favourite love song on the pub jukebox last night
We stayed in the club till gone two o'clock last night
Strong words from her I didn't want to hear last night
Confirmed my worst fears last night
Told me there was someone new, someone I knew, last night
Only fair I should want to know just who, last night
Russ from number two, not just a friend, a lover too, last night
Got through a bottle of our favourite wine last night
Told me the baby wasn't mine last night
She told me she wanted to finish it last night
What we had was gone, she admitted it last night
She rolled me one of her cigarettes and lit it last night
I said it's only one year since we met isn't it, last night
I begged her to tell me exactly why last night
I said I want the truth not a pack of lies, last night
She dealt me a crushing blow, and how, last night
I felt we had something, though not now, since last night
Too late to catch the last bus, she said wait, I'll ask Russ to pick us up, last night
Saw his flashy car, said I'll walk, it's not that far, last night
I had no credit on my mobile phone last night,
The last text she'd sent, I read it, on my lone hike home last night.

Andy MacDonald

Waiting Room

Here we are again, as you lie on the floor,
At the side of my chair, your lead lying slack,
Just one look at you, it's no wonder
We were asked to sit at the back.

I felt it was the least that we could do,
Because you're not too strong in the knees,
And they didn't want the other pets put out,
Nor frightened, nor infected with fleas.

Cos now you're old, and you're toothless,
You're half-deaf and you're half-blind,
All of which I can put up with:
It's the incontinence that I mind.

You're becoming increasingly forgetful,
You just look puzzled, you old wretch.
And you stop halfway to the stick:
You've forgotten what you were going to fetch.

You've become an economic burden,
And now that you're not very well,
You're neither use nor ornament,
And, on top of all that, you smell.

So here we are for your last journey,
The end of the road for you as a pet.
The lifeforce of you will soon be ended,
By that needle in the hands of the vet.

So don't you look up at me like that,
With those big, brown, trusting eyes.
I'm sure you can see into my purpose,
This visit is one way – it can't be disguised.

You've grown up with me and the children,
You've always been faithful and loyal.
You've put in your years of good service,
And to us you've been a friend quite royal.

Dammit, everybody loves you,
Though you're a toothless old hound.
You're just a part of the furniture –
I think that it's time we turned round.

Let's leave this deathly waiting room,
Let's walk right out calm and steady.
You don't need to be pushed into this,
We can do it when I'm finally ready.

Andy Fawthrop

LISTEN

Bleak not to hear birdsong
So clear;
A babbling brook in
Some shady nook,
Rustling leaves,
Crisp and crunchy.
Wind, howling and wailing, rain,
Lashing on the windowpane.
You, safe and snug.
Cocooned and feeling smug.
A frozen, frosty snap,
A twig's sharp, short, crack.
Soft whispering of gentle breeze
Caressing tenderly the sapling trees.
Desperate prattle of the lonely,
Sadness betrayed by speech full-blown.
Human contact is their aim,
To let them down, is a shame.
We go through life so quickly,
With such a lot of beauty to see.
Many things we want to do,
Yet just one, we must see through.

Listen!

Marie Black

GREY

What makes the toilet paper damp?
I wonder, as I break a piece to wipe his mouth.
Propped up in bed,
A vision in cloth and corduroy
On better days.
The plump white rolls sit on the radiator.

Ten years ago,
He might have been able to stand it.
Today, with hands in knots, it's not so easy
When he speaks in garbles,
And the froth of spit
Sometimes
Graces a shoulder.
Well-wishers remain concerned, while wiping with a handkerchief
A little bit
Disgusted.
But, they persevere.
Because,
His words are not of lighter days,
Or times he climbed a plastic slide,
Likely at the age of thirty
Just to reach his lover's
Lost stiletto.
Maybe,
He's forgotten?
I wonder as I sit with him
In his paper room
Of paper lamps.
The world at his pyjama feet.
Enjoying the pillow's cold a bit too much.
Now, he has all the grace of a merry Merman;
When the lampshade spots the ghosts
That sit under his eyelids.
And he winces,
When there's a weight placed on his head;
Thinking it's some shoddy helmet,
From who knows where,
Or what's-his-name.

Though he has the knack
For soup and bread,
Sometimes, the spoon
Akin to soap,
The lavender one he so despises,
Shakes him loose
And makes me mop him. But,
Today I thought,
I'll hold his hand when eating,
Sleeping
Maybe tomorrow
But
You never know.
Actually,

I never did.

Outside there is a bird.
Its grey reminds me of his hair.

Stacey Busuttil

JUDD

My ginger-haired, spirit warrior,
Kind of heart, man and soldier,
Gracious yet strong, you carry me,
You hold me close, yet set me free.
Soften much my inner soul,
You make me one, you make me whole,
Eyes of affection, shine so blue,
Tell me of your love, so true.
Passionate, fiery, tempers wild,
You tame within my inner child.
In your arms, my head's at rest,
Tears we cry and tears we jest.
My angel, my dagger, sword and shield,
You battle for me, our love is sealed,
Forever cherished, tied as one,
United in passion until day is done.

Jessica Williamson

My Valentine

I stand afar with baited breath
    My heart pounding within my chest,
To catch a glimpse, is all I ask
    Alas, what pain to a simple task.

I will not speak or make it known
    She is my queen without a crown,
Her face so vivid within my mind
    Oh cruel world, thou art so unkind.

So fair of skin and eyes so deep
    My poor heart aches, even whilst I sleep.
Hair so blonde and lips so fine
    I know, I know, she cannot be mine.

Thus I stand alone with baited breath
    My heart still throbs within my chest,
Our ages differ, the gap, so vast,
    To catch a glimpse, is, all I ask.

David Richards

Love Is Eternal

We don't always know where to go from here
Especially when the one we love isn't near
But though you may be many miles apart
As long as you love them they're in your heart.

There's no one can take that away from you
However hard they try or what they may do
It just sets your loved ones firmly in place
And always puts a secret smile on your face.

Remember this when you feel lost and alone
Whichever path you choose to walk along
The choices are easy, just feel them and see
That true love stays with you, eternally.

Monica Partridge

ASPECTS OF *Love* - A Collection Of Poetry

MOTHER

The following is what I have learned from you . . .
When you allowed your apron strings to be untied . . .
Like the umbilical cord cut at birth;
I became free to be myself like a bird flown from the nest.
To set goals, to become a professional artist, poet, writer, photographer.
Be happy and to find kindness is in sharing a smile.
And, to be secure enough to love myself, and others is wisdom.
If this is misunderstood by anyone, not my problem , but, the other person.
Mother, you have allowed me to flower from a girl to a woman with my own qualities.
And, I treasure all the past times shared together, remembering now some in my best interest that I did not understand at the time
Mother, as you gracefully become older,
May you be aware of all the positive elements in raising us seven children with care.
It is great to know and realize that we are here for one another no matter what,
An email away.
And, daughter
I never meant to upset nor, anger you in the past.
But, from your voice, I heard your hurt did last.
This negative feeling inside try to let go.
And, only have love in your veins to flow.
A proud parent I have become.
I must say, Shree, well done.

Kathy Carr

GOODBYE SULTAN (14YR OLD GOLDEN COCKER SPANIEL)

The fuschia buds still bobble in the breeze, and everything is almost the same.
The laveteria's filled with humming bees; yet – we'll never more call out his name . . .
The ghosts of summers past will haunt me now; that flash of 'kipper' playing on the lawn
His fourteen summers banked in memory – and I am left alone to feel forlorn . . .

'Each time we say "goodbye" we die a little' – still, his life was just as happy as could be –
And there'll be summers new I can enjoy – the one big difference –
Now there's only me . . .

Edna Sparkes

CRYING!

Let me kiss your tears away
And brush the stains from your cheeks,
What can I say
You are so beautiful,
If I owned the world
I'd give it away to stop you crying,
To stop you feeling sad.
It is day time so all is well,
Let me hold you in my arms
To banish away your fears,
I am proud and strong,
But deep inside me,
Don't tell anyone else,
I feel love incomparable,
Now it is night-time and I come alive.
In the darkness
Love is forgotten, I feel the need to be alive,
Then in the shadows I walk
Any sensitivity I had is gone,
Beware for I can be so cruel and violent
You would think I was made of two separate souls.

Craig Bumpus

I LOVE YOU

The words drowning out the sounds,
Why, would I rather listen than to learn,
Song is so sad,
But yet . . . it feels right.

The night, seems so close,
Even though the sun is so high,
Me and you dancing under the light of the moon,
Showing me your magnificent face.

The words escape my mind,
When I want to tell you how much you mean
To me, you wrapped in our arms,
My eyes fixed upon yours.

Sparkling under the light, I'm stuck like glue,
Three words baby . . . I love you.

Kyle Winstone-Evans

I Was Alive

I was alive
But you breathed life into me.
I had no emotion
But now I feel everything.
I did not know the world existed,
But now I feel the sun and rain.
I was an island
Now I am the universe.
I was empty
But you have filled me.
You touch me
With an easiness that comes so naturally.
I look into your eyes
And I am weak.
You smile and I am lost,
Your laughter fills my head,
And I am drunk.
You have etched yourself into my life
And engraved your name into my soul.

John Howe

Absent Love

And in my mind do you so clearly appear
Snapshots of memory, creating DNA for a dreamy life existence in my head
Through imagination I can talk to you, anticipate your response,
See you laugh and hold that cheeky smile
I can undress you and trace fingers over imagined contours
We can walk Heaven together, claiming sunset and sunrise

But . . .

How will I know the comfort of arms around me, warm and secure?
Where are the answers to questions I don't understand?
When will I feel the electric thrill of shared space?
Where can I look to find a true reflection of a humbled self?
When will I really know me, know you, know us?

Not through an imagined scenario or storyline
Not through the misty lens of an eye and a memory.
But simply by you being here.

Sharon Waring

TIME REVERSED

The years apart led us in different directions, our lives filled with creation and escapade, ups and downs, experiences too many to mention.

Where in my body did your memory reside? Nowhere but in my heart, as the thought of you I could never push aside.

The distance seems minuscule and insignificant as we share thoughts from across the seas, listening to your voice, enjoying our laughter; it's as if you never did leave.

What is the point of thinking of time or love lost, when you are here now, never to leave again, a friendship to keep at all cost.

I remember you well, like it was yesterday that I said goodbye, if I said I didn't miss you, think of you, long for you, it would all be a lie.

You are here now, back in my life to occupy the space that is yours.
You are here now to fill the void.
How we wish we could allow nature to take its course

A new life begins, or more so one renewed, a life with a meaning, a peace ensued.

I say welcome back, have a seat, relax and enjoy the ride, as you absorb the journey, take a moment to think of how I feel inside.

Every fibre of every cell and muscle speaks of overwhelming joy and elation, my heart, soul and mind all stand at attention.

A tribute to you, words I hope are fitting, welcome back to my heart, a place where you forever will be sitting.

Thomas Hudson

IN YOUR REACH

One human upon a world,
that is so small from the outside.
A distant unknown but I,
am chosen by you *my knight*.
In a dream that makes everything,
so much *brighter than it was before*.
Reality struck me when
we stood together on the grass lawn.
For the first time in my life
I felt above all the danger
in a world that seemed so long ago.
Back then you were but a *stranger*.

I am now facing *the best thing*
that had ever happened to me,
in a life that was so dark.
You bare a light of love so free.
So pure that just a thought
of being without that *feeling* you
give me, makes tears break the surface.
Yet still our *love* is revealing.
It's not just my hand or my eyes,
my mind or my kiss that brings release.
For I am sure now of one thing,
for ever is my heart in your reach.

Nikita Liebscher

DEAR JOHN

The postman called long years ago
I knew what he would say
'The king requests your company
For two years to the day.'

My sweetheart then-a comely blonde
Said 'Never fear, Dear John
I love you, so we will not part
Our love is far too strong.'

So off I went to serve the king
And left my love behind
But we wrote letters every day
The sweet and gentle kind.

Then her letters petered out
No longer sweet and caring
Until at last 'Dear John' arrived
Her reasons she was sharing.

Two years she said was far too long
To keep our love alight
Another lad had come along
And put it all to flight

And so she wrote to say goodbye
Those many years ago
But unrequited love it seems
Takes many years to go.

Robert John Ponting

Sonnet To A Winter Garden

My love's lost song alone to her I sang,
each note and chord aloft as wing'ed tears,
that one soft tone fresh from my heartbreak sprang,
might light perchance upon those wanton ears;
There on, to flow, a single salted prayer,
to fall, if chanced, upon that ice-bound heart;
Bestowed; its tender, tragic warmth to share,
and prise those bitter hoar-struck bonds apart.
Set free, let flow that hotly passioned blood,
and melting, set each frozen vein afire,
to scarlet bloom each ice-encrusted bud,
made blossom in that Eden of desire.

And in that garden; rediscover yet,
love's tender song must needs be sung duet.

Sullivan The Poet

Taken

I'm so taken by you
and you know this
Or at least you can feel
or even sense it
in my manner, whenever you are around
Oh how I simply do whatever you ask
just because it's what you want
regardless of what I receive in return
Although . . .
what I do receive is a smile, some laughter
and a sense of relief from you
that I am around
I am your living favour
that you never have to return

Michael McArdle

MY VALENTINE

I've loved you since the first day we met
Those many long years ago.
Through the trials and tribulations
My love has continued to grow.

From the moment you pushed me out of my seat
On the bus to sit with my dad
Cos you wanted to sing, as always did he
And I was just a lad.

We held hands as we walked up to school
And looked into each other's eyes.
It's easy to think it was just puppy love
But I knew I'd captured a prize.

And later when we became engaged
At midnight that Christmas Eve.
We exchanged our rings and promised our love
I knew I could never you leave.

Then through the years, as my work took us all
To many different places.
You never complained at the problems that gave
You just made friends with all the new faces.

When our daughter arrived, we were both ecstatic
And your mothering instincts came out.
You handled it all with your usual aplomb
Of your love there was never a doubt.

And when she was married, you stood by her side
As proud as any mother could be.
You held me so tight, as you fought back the tears
It made me quite weak at the knee.

And now as we're older, and it's grandsons we cherish
The love that we've shared makes me glad.
I still love that girl with the beautiful curl
Who came and sat next to my dad.

Ian Lumley

A POEM OF LOVE

We sat on the roof the whole night through,
By the light of the silvery moon.
'Oh, how I long to marry you,
And may that day come soon.'

We raised our voices to the stars,
We did not care who heard us,
Nor when they shouted loud and clear,
'For God's sake stop that fuss!'

We met at a party, some months ago,
Across the room our eyes had met.
I loved you then, at just one glance,
And always will, my pet.

But you were with another beau,
And so were not alone.
Though when the evening ended,
It was I who saw you home.

The course of true love does not run smooth.
I had a rival, from next door.
Who said that you belonged to him.
So I knocked him to the floor!

And now the wedding day is nigh.
I almost shed a tear.
For I am such a lucky guy,
To care for you, my dear.

I'll take you away in a pea-green boat,
And I'll sing to my small guitar,
What a beautiful pussy you are, you are,
What a beautiful pussy you are.

Eve M Turner

THIRTEEN SITE

A service camp in sixty-one
With all its square cut lines
I will remember always
But not for drink or wines
But for the love that came to me
From one who really cared.
Who showed me deep sincerity
And how it should be shared
Who took my hand and led me
Through a strange and delicate world
Where the spoken word is stardust
Where the silver lining curled
And two blend gently into one
Such happiness will soon be gone
Come cast away convention's shrouds
To walk with me among the clouds
The jealous gods forbid most mortals
To wander through their lofty portals.

Robert Stevens

MORE THAN WORDS CAN SAY

Think of all the raindrops that have
Fallen on this Earth
Imagine they are diamonds
Then you will know your worth
Think of all the works of art
That we shall ever see
They fade like petals of a flower
Compared my love to thee
Imagine all the words of love
The world has ever known
Tied up with a golden cord
And then to the Heaven thrown
When the angels read them
I know they will agree
That no one in this whole wide world
Could love you more than me.

Joyce Chaffer

Old Letters In A Chest

Past loves,
lost lives
reconstructed history.

Fragmented half-charred memories,
familiar yet no less strange

Personal history of lonely isolation.
Incomprehensible feelings –
the foreign language of forgotten departures.

Groundhog day destinations.
The sickening turbulence of recognition.

Hindsight and explanation become
more
and less
true with air miles of time.

The particulate entropy of private moments
laid bare but encrypted.

Urgently required
an individual code-breaking archivist.

Stephen P B West

Endless Love

Our love is like an endless light
That's glowing wondrously,
Our love is like a free spirit
That's full of energy,
Mysterious you are my love,
My passion burns inside.
And I will love thee until the
Ceasing of the tide,
Until the ceasing of the tide
My love
And beyond the stars and sun
I will love thee still until
The affection of your heart
I have won.

Emma-Louise Gardner

THE TABLE IS MY HEART

The knife without the fork,
The jam without the jar,
The wine without the cork
The table is my heart.

The salt without the pepper
The plate without the food
The chair opposite empty
The table is my mood.

The butter without the bread
Dessert without the spoon
It's spinning round my head
All I need is you.

My sweet, luscious angel cake
The apple of my eye.
The milk on my cornflakes
The pigeon in my pie.

My tablecloth is non-existent
I'm a dog without a bone.
The pattern is, of course, consistent
I'm forever on my own.

Cecilia Neil-Smith

TRUE CALLING

Love untouched by human hand.
Is sung by angel whispers.
To open hearts and open ears
Softly wafting on the breeze
Of conscious vibrations.
Drifting through the senses.
Encircling the being,
Of each recipient
As the welcoming heart
Accepts its true calling.

Marie Erskine

LOVE IS

Love is devotion,
Caring and trust.
Love is not hateful,
Jealous or lust.

Full of forgiveness,
Honest and true.
There's no disbelief,
To make us blue.

From deep in the heart,
Keeping us strong.
No money to pay,
Lasting so long.

Love casts no shadow.
Lights up your way.
Love is the rainbow,
Brightens your day.

Daniel Winter

THE PEARL IN THE OYSTER

Meet my wife
She's my life
I met her quite a while ago
My love for her just grows and grows
The mother of my boys
With beauty, wit and poise
Gives me everything I need
Just one smile is proof indeed
A perfect lover
I don't need no other
She gives me all I want from love
The only one I'm thinking of
She's a wife, a mother and a lover
The pearl in the oyster
I was to discover

David Holmes

NO LOVE LOST

So it's been two weeks since you used the cliché
'It's not you, it's me'
It's really hard to just let that go
And not take it personally.

It would have been nice for you to prove me wrong
And show me that men aren't that bad
But yet again it seems I was right
Which genuinely makes me quite sad

I just don't understand what went wrong
Because we laughed all of the time
Yet I knew deep down when I wasn't there
I was out of sight and out of mind

I wish I'd stayed impartial
Like I said right from the start
But even so, I want you to know
You did not break my heart

It may be slightly dented
And the surface may be scratched
But it didn't take me long to notice
You weren't the perfect catch

You were too fashion-conscious, for a girl like me
Where trackies and hi-tops would do
You own far too many pink shirts for a bloke
You really don't need more than two

I reckon that I was just a toy
You used to relieve your stress
But maybe one day you'll realise
That you just lost one of the best

You won't have banter with another girl
Nor will you love her shoes
She won't be able to DJ like me
Or have an amazing pair of boobs

I hate the way I fell for you
And the fact you made me sad
But the only guy a girl can depend on
Really is her dad.

Jane Baker

IF ONLY

The years and miles between us
Mean we'll never meet.
She in her world
Me in mine
Unless,
Performing some extraordinary feat
Newsworthy I become
Prime time.

So until then I have to be content
To see her lovely face and hear her dulcet tones
At six o'clock upon my TV screen.
Inspiring me with dreams
Of that which might have been.
Or do I?
Have I forgotten?
What was in truth, those years ago,
My lovely wife.
Her limpid eyes, jet-black hair
When I was not so much aware.
A callow youth,
A shallow brain.
We made it work though all the same.
Now four grown-up children later
I want to do it all again.

It's just as well we'll never meet
Dreams and love are shattered by the smell of sweaty feet
The snores at night
And a thousand little things that blight
Perfection in reality
So I'll dream on, this time knowing that I'll never disappoint
Let time take its course and not defer
In purging all these thoughts
Of what it would be like to live with her.
But every now and then
I'll stop awhile
Stretch out a finger and imagine
That I touch that lovely smile.

Ben Corde

Loving Memories

Sunrise creeping forth from the night sky
A beautiful day dawns
Alarms beep, all rise
Relaxing and pampering
Time creeping by

Deep and wondrous red
Pure and gentle white
Beautiful and delicate gifts from nature
A sparkling light with a gentle energy shining through
Reflecting unconditional love to all and you

Pitter-patter of raindrops on the windowpane
No rain today Mr Weatherman if you please
Rain lessens and the sun peaks through
Sunshine through smiles beaming unconditional love at you

Ribbons flying this way and that
Gentle and natural beauty shining through
A proud moment for those closest to you
A glass raised and loving hugs
Calmness and excitement hand in hand
Time has run past

Ribbons flying this way and that
As the gentle breeze whirls past
Ribbons still again, first arrival
Seconds pass, final arrival, all together
The wondrous door is near

A beautiful and gentle church standing proud
A buzz in the air and a few butterflies too
With a deep breath the butterflies flutter by
An exchange of smiles between two

Smiles of love filling the air all joining as one
A thousand eyes smiling at you
Beautiful eyes shining with love
A sharing of words, a joining link
Sunlight streaming through in rainbows
Smiling through songs
Beautiful readings echoing through

ASPECTS OF *Love* - A Collection Of Poetry

Rainbow colours fill the air
Eyes smiling, hearts shining, lighting the sky
Laughter and joy
Clicking and flashing
Memories frozen in time
Love and laughter will always be true

Living, being, enjoying every second of each moment
No awareness of time, time alone tells no story
The air is alight with love and laughter
It is sure to be happily ever after

Clicking and flashing
More memories still
Standing ovation as you walk through
Heartfelt happiness gliding towards, above and around you
Celebration with all encircling you

The sharing of food
Laughter and smiles
A room filled with love
And lots more love shining down from above

Reminiscing through words
Loving words floating and holding true beautiful memories of you
Smiles and laughter
Happy tears falling through
And a few little cringes at times too

Bright lights filling the sky
Symbols of love floating above
More memories frozen in what is time
The moon and the stars shining as part of you

Floating and gliding
A meaningful song
Two reminiscing and smiling
Slowness and gentleness
A few crazy steps added in too

Celebrations continue . . .
All hearts shining with laughter and smiles
Day and night united
The sun to the moon surrounded by stars

Quietening of laughter
Smiles holding true
Celebrations continue as resting draws near
Memories and love locked like gifts in thousands of hearts
All will hold true
In the hearts of all that know you.

Ann Parkinson

DESERT

She was my goddess of India;
Following the Ganges in robes of yellow-red,
Golden bangles clicking on slender wrists,
Nut-brown feet held in jewelled sandals
Camera clicking indiscretions behind closed doors.
She was my light on dark days;
Long brown hair caught up in sequined headdress,
Bambi eyes held wanton desires
Henna-painted hands touching lives
Camera clicking childhood whispers.
She was my ache of a heartbeat;
Soft ruby lips begging to be kissed
Curvaceous body slick with amber oil
Camera clicking with trembling fingers.
She was my happiness of my soul;
Touching me with delicate caress
Climbing to places not yet explored
A gilded magpie with treasure to be found
Camera clicking uncertain tremors.
She was all that I dreamed of in a woman
We should have had forever
Wrong place, wrong time
Camera clicking, bullet cracking
Life ending, hearts breaking.

Amanda Thompson

MOONSTRUCK

How many nights do you remember
That were so beautiful you could cry?
The moonlight, the sound of waves
A place where you could die.

How many nights do you remember
Where the moonlight kissed your lips?
The sand caressed the swelling breast
And your body fondled by fingertips.

How many nights do you remember
A force greater than the sea?
That entered your heart, like a golden dart
And stung you like a bee.

Moira Whittley

LOVE OF THE DANCE

She glanced my way with her laughing eyes,
As my heart missed a beat, to my surprise.
Her hair flowed so long, with its golden hints,
With a freckled nose like autumn tints.

Without a word I took her hand
As we danced into this other land,
Where love was all, as I held her tight
We flowed with the music of the night.

The dance of love had just begun,
I knew she was mine for we danced as one.
She swayed as I held her cheek to mine,
I looked at her face, and saw her eyes shine.

With her laughing eyes she looked his way,
He just took her hand and led her away.
With her golden hair and her freckled nose,
He too saw love, as my heart closed.

I was sure that I saw her love for me,
Now she's gone and has love for all to see.
The love of the dance just took her away.
But the look in her eyes will always stay.

Barbara Leswell

LOVE AT FIRST SIGHT

In April nineteen eighty five, friends like her were few,
I saw her in the Automart, and with a mate I went to view.
She lived in Newton-le-Willows at a large newsagent's shop,
With no time to spare, we hit the road, there wasn't time to stop.

By the time of our arrival, late on Sunday afternoon,
The daylight gradually fading with a lovely silver moon.
As we turned the final corner there she stood beneath a tree,
And the second I clapped eyes on her, I knew that she's for me.

I walked into the paper shop, hyped up and full of glee,
The lady behind the counter chucked her keys across to me
Take her for a spin she said, hey! I don't mind if I do,
And I knew full well she'd soon be mine, that lovely XR2.

Her bodywork was grimy, her white paint all sad and dull,
I started up her engine and her fuel gauge read half full.
I checked her brakes and steering, and finally her clutch,
And thinking she's a dream come true, I liked her very much.

As I drove out on the highway, she felt steady as a rock,
My lovely new found partner had low mileage on her clock.
Her engine's sweet as candy, her gearbox so precise,
And everything about her I thought was really nice.

She was up at three two fifty, but I offered him three grand,
He stood there silent for a sec, and then he shook my hand.
I can't describe the feeling, when a final deal was struck,
And heading on the long drive home, I couldn't believe my luck.

It took a couple of weekends, but she polished to pristine,
I changed her oil and filter, and give her engine bay a clean.
I fettled up her greasy bits, and shampooed all her trim.
To have the coolest car in town, for me's a personal whim.

If I could have just one thing back from any of my past,
I don't need to think, she'd be the one, my love for her was vast.
She just looked so outstanding and oozing tons of sex,
I wish I'd never let her go WBA 200X.

Philip Boote

TWO LOVERS

A wedding took place in a church long ago,
The groom was resplendent, the bride was aglow.
They had known each other since ringlets and curls,
She was the pick of the bunch; amongst all other girls.
He tried many ways to impress her; no doubt,
When he succeeded, inside he would shout.

There's pleasure and pain in courtship and love,
But if the god Eros smiles down from above,
Both hearts will entwine and love will ensue,
With trust, dedication; both must be true.

Time just moves on, and lovers do too,
In the mid nineteen fifties, it was me; it was you.
I tried to impress you in so many ways,
I loved you, I left you and counted the days
We took to resole the situation: no doubt.
Perhaps[s that's what true love is really about.

There's pleasure and pain in courtship and love,
But when the god Eros smiles down from above,
Both hearts will entwine and love will ensue,
With trust, dedication; both must be true.

The years are unfolding toward the next century
Unknown the adventures that still are to be.
As lovers have continued through all of the ages
We too; will have our story, in history's pages.

I love you still, of that there's no doubt,
That's what true love is really about.
There's pleasure and pain in courtship and love,
But because the god Eros smiled down from above,
Both hearts have entwined and love did ensue.
With trust: dedication
Both have been true.

Jim Spain

The Procrastinator

It was you who fell first, while I lost my footing
You said that I was the fairest
The promises we made I thought were to keep
But our first kiss, it was so careless

I don't see why not, you assured with a smile
Buttons parted and I was delirious
I guess I knew at the back of my mind
Except I was in love and fearless

I don't see why not, you shrugged when I asked
Like a man who's asked what he's thinking
But you must have known at the back of your mind
Just as I, that we were sinking

You dropped my heart while I was still laughing
Look, you said, there's nothing there
And the tightrope I walked wobbled and broke
So I let go and fell through the air

We were not made to last, I should never have asked
I should never have waited 'til later
Now I wait alone but I forgive myself
Love had space in the procrastinator

Fiona Pearse

Love

Love is patient, love is kind, it has no enemies
It perseveres in the face of adversity – it never gives up
Love listens, understands and consoles
Love does not run away when unhappiness knocks on the door
It will stand and fight for that which is right
Love knows no nationality, it has no flag, no anthem yet it is shared by all
Love will support, encourage and inspire
It is not vain or boastful save in God
Were it not for love, life would cease to have meaning
Love will protect those most dear and always show compassion
It is in loving and forgiving that people are healed.

Derek Dobson

WEEP NO MORE

My love, no longer must you weep,
Though I have gone, I'm not asleep.
I'm with you still, in every way,
I am my love, with you today.

I am the summer breeze that blows,
The wonder of those winter snows,
Each sparkling star you see at night,
I am my love, within your sight.

I am the sunlight on ripened grain,
I am the gentle autumn rain,
I am each golden grain of sand,
I am the one who holds our hand.

So my love, no longer cry,
Though not here, I did not die.

Len A Hynds

INVISIBLE

I purse my lips
I flounce my hips
Alas, it's all in vain
For though my eyes seek only you
Yours never will seek mine

I frown, I cry
I stamp my feet
And all to no avail
For though my heart belongs to you
You never gave me yours

Nicola Brooks-Williamson

GYPSY BOY

Gypsy boy where have you been
With brawny hands and body lean,
Saw you walking down the street
With shoulder sway and dance on feet.
As you spoke my heart went warm
To eyes of fire the soul was drawn,
Gypsy boy you've taken my mind
I want more of the Romany kind.
Surely you walk in the shadow of the sun
I feel with you life could be fun,
Living in a fairy ring
With golden meadows and lark bird sing!
Moon bathing in wild waters blue
In fish darting ripples with transparent hue.
I'm dancing in haystacks embracing breeze
Lying in your arms under talking trees.

Gypsy boy let's take the road
With arch-caravan light of load.
While away time with pallet and brush
Skins will tan a bronzer blush.
Gypsy boy you make my heart sing
My arms around you I want to fling.
I want to gallop beaches, feel sea pray on my face,
Ride bareback let the wild heart race!
Tame the untamed horse with windblown mane
Gallop where rivers start, to the higher plane.
Higher and higher, where Indians still roam free!

Back to roots – pure poetry
Passion in my eager heart grows
You look so cool in true gypsy pose.
With the dawn I tersely awaken
You wear the ring; your heart's been taken.

Vera Tyrer Collins

SPECIAL DATE

19th of the 3rd, 11.
Were a match made in Heaven
This is my way of letting you know
No matter what happens,
My love for you will always show
Without you, there's no sparkle in my eyes
No smile on my face and no special prize
Together always and I hope you think it too
Because nothing can change
How much I love you.
We have a baby on the way
This brightens up our lives, not just our day
Our little baby Leo
I guess you can say, we will make the perfect trio.
I've got to admit,
Your smile is driving me crazy
It's like a drug that can always amaze me
You're the best thing that's happened in my life
And one day for sure I'll be your wife
When my mother passed away
Everything turned black and grey
But when I met you, it was untrue
Because everything turned bright and blue
And baby that's one reason why I love you.

Katie Elizabeth Howell

The First Kiss

The first time I ever saw you
I fell in love straight away
You looked straight at me and smiled
Your fair hair fell gently across your face.

The first time you spoke to me
I went quiet and shy
I just didn't know what to say to you
So you started this conversation by asking my name.

The first time that you touched me
Sent shivers down my spine
Your hand accidentally got tangled with mine
But we both held on longer than we needed.

Linda Casey

A Mum In A Million

My mum, she is perfect
She is wonderful and a loving mum
She has a heart of gold
And has a happy heart
She is a sensitive person
She likes to help her friends and family
My mum is truly a great help.

My mum takes after her dad
My grandad Eric
I take after my mum and my grandad Eric
My mum is a part of me in many ways
We are both caring
We share and we think of other people
We help each other.

My mum is the biggest part in my life
She brought me up as a child
While suffering with learning difficulties and a disability
My mum has always been here for me

I love you, Mum.

Tom Brealey

Hidden Love

I smiled sweetly and quickly turned away
Etching the image of your face onto my memory
I wanted to turn around and smile again at you
But then you would know how much I yearned for you
The first time that our eyes had met
My heart seemed to leap, and my eyes could hardly believe
That one man could be so utterly gorgeous
You were everything I dreamt and hoped for in a man
And best of all was that you were kind, funny and sexy, too
I have always loved you since that first glance
But no reaction came from you, you turned and walked away
Since then, each day we would see each other during our working day
You'd tell a joke, politely wave, or briefly stop on by
One night whilst working late to get a deadline through
Who should slowly come behind, so quietly
And without a word was you
Your arms went around my waist and startled, I swiftly turned
Our eyes met first and then our lips
I'm sure I floated off the floor
After our embrace, I smiled sweetly and told you how I felt
You smiled back sexily and held both my hands
And said from the start you always knew
Now since our first encounter, our nights are spent together
Wrapped in each other's arms, still smiling sweetly.

Julianne Clarke

Her Book Of Cold Spells

Moonbeams awake again and the lunar muse has cracked into the mind like electricity.
This morning the pen scribbles because thighs of a poet are bound in tight belt of blue,
A witch had locked his belt some barren desert drifting, shifting years ago, kept the key,
She was a sparrow, sad and chaste like her whispering book of charms and cold spells,
Sort of disembodied and exorcised with no body because her soul had long flown away,
A curse was cast in her heart so she had to gouge mine out with crazy cardiac surgery.
If I was ticked again by love it would not be with a sparrow, but a dark raven swooping.

Nigel Pearce

You Cannot Hate Hate Until You Love Love

If Man would think decisions through,
The world would change each day,
With simple words like 'I love you!'
Based on Christ's words to pray . . .
For Man can choose the higher path,
God's more excellent way,
Despite the fact that scoffers laugh,
Refusing to obey . . .

If Man would seek the Lord each time
A brand new day begins,
The world would see less pain, less crime,
Less horrors and less sins . . .
For Man is more than just one life,
Ask Christ, God's precious Prince,
He conquered death, its sting, its strife,
In Him, each Christian wins . . .

If Man would set aside his hate,
Forgiveness as the norm,
Then love would be the finest state
To which he could conform . . .
For Man can cool his heels with prayers,
Beyond the present storm,
To recognise that God still cares,
With steadfast love so warm . . .

If Man could learn the Gospels well,
What miracles we'd see,
With prophecies that would foretell
God's greatest mystery . . .
For Man forgiven, humbled, learns
From Christ and Calvary . . .
Awaiting Christ, when He returns
To rule with majesty!

Denis Martindale

To My Darling

The roaring sound of the deep blue sea
To me is like a symphony
That goes on through eternity
And sings of my love for thee.

The roaring sound of the autumn wind
Is the greatest orchestration
It stirs the thoughts within my mind
And fires my imagination.

I imagine being by the sea
With the autumn wind in my hair
I imagine you to be with me
And love being everywhere.

Ernest-Wilhelm Peters

Sonnet For My Love

What love of mine with eyes so blue,
Like pools of sapphires that seek to draw me in,
Would gaze at me and my love grow anew?
Content to lie wrapped in the sheets of sin.
Could I not resist such devilish charms,
Though thrust upon me by a handsome shape?
Alas! I perceive he will do no harm,
And inside his warm embrace I am draped.
Oh my sweet how your lips call me to them,
As gentle and kind as I could wish for.
My soulmate and my most precious of gems.
King of my heart, in my thoughts evermore.
To hold and to cherish, forever mine.
My one and only, till the day we die.

Charlotte Crisp

Forbidden

I know I'm not your Juliet.
I know it can't be so.
Like Echo I'll
Repeat your name
Until I pine away.
Like Niobe weep a waterfall,
Burn for you each day.
Innocent, with your
Bitter sweet
Naivety, you'd try
Comfort me
But never
See
In me, what you're looking for.
For me it's easy, you're
All. I want and more. Much more.

You're my Vodka, in this, prolonged
Prohibition.
Too potent, heady and
So I hanker after.
Meet your eyes;
My face in flames
Shamed burst of love.

Talk about you – more than often,
As though I
Like the shape, as your name, it forms upon my lips,
I
Like the sound of it, dancing on my tongue's very
Tip.

I fear one day, my
Face will betray
The obsession running. Through my veins.
They can't know; *you*
Can't know; I'm
Forbidden.
To love you.
Bound by situation
Forbidden. Relation.

Can't confess
To you.
You smile at me but
My heart.
You look

Through.

Hannah Dickinson

A Place Of Rest For You

I will make a place of rest for you, kind;
Free from the gallows of your tortured mind,
And spiteful tongues, those so inclined unwind.

Perhaps belated, justice of a sort for borrow,
Awaits, a harbor for lost time and dreamed tomorrow,
Once cuffed to coppiced thoughts of deepest sorrow.

A place befitting, for wrongs bestowed upon your brow
Of callous castings, so this soul did bear, till now,
Once lost behind the coldest walls, interred somehow.

Festered wounds did laminate an unjust finding,
Life's clock, no joyous hands through all their winding,
In time, back then and now may lose their binding.

Soar free to naked virgin ground, sits here for you.
A play, in time for man and mind to make anew,
To grow in earth, new heart, though years are few.

Is best, this place of rest and peace that I have found.
Where walls of limestone, lay dry, ordered over ground,
Now all is silent, passed, there is no sound.

I have made a place of rest for you, kind.
Sit here beside you, listening, just to ease your mind,
Gone, spiteful tongues, for someone else to find.

This place befitting, to watch a smile without a borrow.
Words of comfort, finds this soul with hope, tomorrow;
Now found, to feel the warmth, without a sorrow.

A place of rest for you.

Michael Bracken

TO DREAM OF GOLD

Here stands the statue,
Thorn-poked, storm-cloaked.
He has no rest, metal pressed
On my art-damaged, heart-ravaged mind;
I am savage.
Sit close and watch my pen draw blood.

In black dressed rain
Your brambles fall like glass-shards
The name of my house driven once more into the dirt.
I pay my debts;
Storm the castle with heart-red sword,
Following the golden line that spells these words.

I am so small in your bed,
A trembling of weaknesses.
Sleeplessness; her alchemy fled,
Cast your runes to raise the dead.

And I, bronze,
Despite her, despise myself,
I miserly beg
To have and hold
This creature spun
From red and white gold.

Nicolas Bowyer

LAMENT

The way we were is not the way we are.
Gone are the days of ecstasy,
When a touch could light a flame
Of anticipated delight.
Then we lay contented,
Satisfied by its flame.
It was a transient thing,
That quietly slipped away.
We were left bereft,
Lamenting the way we were,
Not the way we are.

Tony Ellis

Untitled

As you venture out,
On your own,
Remember son,
You're not alone.

Although you've grown up,
And you're moving out,
Your mum and I are here,
Just give us a shout.

We've always done our best,
To help and protect you,
Even when it felt
Like we were hurting you.

We won't be around forever,
But when we depart,
Know we're still with you,
Alive in your heart.

Catherine Butterfield

Il Mio Unico Vero Amore

When I look into your eyes,
I feel my fears melt away,
Nights are not as threatening,
My gaze, it cannot stray.

Your arms are my protection,
Keeping me safe while we rest,
But things are falling apart,
Can our love stand this test?

A smile spreads across my lips,
As you call my name,
You've turned my life around,
Nothing can ever be the same.

You've touched my heart,
Released my desires,
Brought me out of myself,
But can we do what the other requires?

Lauren Brazier

Ode To A Portrait

Come tomorrow, you would have been fifty,
I, at sixty, grown old in your mem'ry;
God willed that you be e'er young at forty.
He took you in prime of womanhood,
Vibrant, fragrant bloom suddenly frozen.

But every time I look at your portrait
That prominently rests on that mantel,
You come alive and commune with my soul.
The vibrant cheer that radiates from your face
Lifts up my spirit from depressive mire;
The gentle smile that hovers round your lips
Is tender as it ever was in warmth;
But most of all it is your eyes that hold
Me thralled by their sheer mesmeric allure
As I sit hours on end in mem'ries lost
Of our rollicking times of fun together –
The tinkling peals of your infectious laughter
The pit-pat of your feet around the house
Your pouts of sulking moods of cyclic blues
The dulcet melody of your sweet voice
Yells of annoyance at petty trifles –
All these and more come crowding in my mind.

Thus I eke out my lone years on Earth
In a world of our own fantasy
Basking in the sunshine of your portrait
Impatient for that day when we will be
United in that land beyond the river
Drenched in eternal bliss ne'er more to part.

Dr Nithie Victor

Broken Fairytale

A tiny flickering flame in an ocean of dark
A beautiful fairytale child still emitting a spark.
The joy of new life, the abyss of new death
And the time in-between you spent fighting for breath.
Fly away little princess,
No more pain, no more fears,
We'll stumble on through the haze of tears.
A single snowflake, a drop of rain
A fairy tale smashed and shattered in pain.
But your struggle for life was never in vain
You're eternally part of us now, Ellie Jane.

Stephanie Edwards

To Ros

My love for you is sure, and strong as death,
So faithful, ever constant, firm and pure,
It will survive as long as I have breath,
And then outlive my life and still endure.
To such a love there cannot be an end,
It came so late in life, and yet it came,
But when did love to time or age attend?
It only cares that love is worth the name.
You do not even know how much I care,
And will not know until my life is through,
Although to speak my love I do not dare,
It will be there for ever, strong and true,
You, ever in my thoughts, there is no doubt,
My lips are silent, but my heart cries out.

Bill Fletcher

PRISON OF LOVE

I am ruled by my two jailers
Imprisoned by their charms
In patterned regulation
The times and tides laid down
They cannot be resisted in our diurnal rounds
In return I have their loyalty, love and missing socks
I am imprisoned by my love of these two dogs.

Ernest Roberts

LOVE SICK AND SICK OF LOVE

He's just dragged me through a rose garden, backwards and upside down . . .
Smells sweet but the thorns have pricked me all over

I'm out of bandages to mend my heart
And no doctor can stitch up the cracks
For the tears that pour out
It will leave me drained.

I want my love again
But my head can't take the stress
And my heart has a thousand stitches
Ridden with love lost

I have an internal ache
It's because I crave
An unconditional discovery
An awakening mystery

I'm love sick
And sick of love
But I've craved it so much
For so long
I'm not sure I could do without its touch!

Dee Makanda

ANNA

Walking together
Down Trinity Road
Me taking you to the train station
Seeing you off.
Wishing
I could kiss you
Goodbye.

Later
Walking together
Along Nantucket Avenue
To the store
On Wyse Road.
Wishing
I could kiss you
Goodbye
As you board the bus.

Later again
Sitting together
In Oshawa;
Wishing
We could be alone.

The next day
We are
Yet we leave
So much unsaid;
Speaking volumes
In our unspoken love.
Then
I wish
I had not
Kissed you

Goodbye.

I loved/love you Anna
I always will.

Whoever
I may be with.

Frank Pavitt

All Loved Up – Hers

Hey – guess what? How about that?
We've moved into our very own flat
A couple's space – it's rather swish
A trial for marriage is what I wish.

Four weeks on – sweet sheer bliss
We're still locked in a honeymoon kiss
Apart from smelly socks on the floor
I really couldn't ask for more

It's somehow changed – he gets on my wick
He slurps his tea – it makes me sick
I thought I loved him like no other
Why am I forced to visit his mother?

His mates come round, parties are loud
Why does he need such a big crowd?
Not my scene – I'm off to bed
Remember the loving words he said

Six months in, things are tense
He still hasn't fixed the garden fence
Toe nails in the bath, always on the phone
Football on the telly, then there's that loan . . .

The rent's due, we've bills to pay
He's never in – it's special today
I've made a nice birthday meal
But he's late, a troubled car wheel

He never stops snoring at night
I'm so fed up of all these fights
If he shouts at me again like that
I'll walk out and never come back.

All these arguments make me sad
I wish I'd stayed with Mum and Dad
He says I'm a nagging boring moaner
Well he is one big awful groaner

The leak needs fixing, he always forgets
Just like us, damaged with neglect
All loved up, together forever
Now we simply discuss the weather

We didn't last – over in a year
I've shed a bucket full of tears
Onto John – a brand new fella
This time it'll be so much better . . .

Sharon Boothroyd

ICU

I saw your face:
Dark, where the eyes are.
The deep bridge of nose,
the swell of the chin.

The tiny hairs that line
the top of the mouth.
Your teeth even, white
as if magnified.

Your breath licked at me
caught on the sensory path
to the brain. An anticipatory
pause.

The dark edge of water
in the autumnal lake:
The heartache.

It wasn't instant:
This knowledge,
the gratification. Pause

for more and more
until
the leaves fall all rusty.
The colours reflected.
A joy so bright
in orange, red and gold;
taut as the veins are
under the skin.

Trace the words:
All the ways I . . .
in liquid fire.

Rosalind J Lee

CRIES FROM A CHILD'S HEART

I cannot say if I will love again
If I should, I would be so careful not to harm that
Precious heart or cause it pain.
As mine was bruised and all alone when my daddy left
All my life I have felt bereft
Time goes by, I am still that child, bewildered,
Part lost.
He could not have known what his leaving home
Had cost.
The ache the empty space inside
Through the years I have often cried
Sad to say that no one has really filled my heart
The space was his and so I let my life go by with
Wasted loves, wasted all.

Elizabeth Morton

MY DREAM MAN

I imagine a tall, dark, handsome man
Who will touch my heart with no plan
He should have sparkly light eyes
Charming smile to curb my appetites
He should be soft spoken gentleman
Carry himself confidently, also is intelligent
He should have strong muscles to embrace me tight
A fit body proudly graced, protect me from any sight
He should be millionaire or even a billionaire
Buy me diamonds, handle me with great care
He should help people in needy
But should not be a greedy
He should be someone special to seek
Make my knees shiver and voice weak
He should make my heart beat really fast
Believe me I will love him deeply till the world last.

Farzana Nadeem

THY VALENTINE QUEEN

Thy Valentine Queen,
Announcing victories,
While bedazzling the world,
O greatest female,
O greatest champion,
O greatest heroine,
Enjoy your Valentine's Day,
With romantic memories
Celestial and divine,
Inside the Senate of Rome,
Beside the fountain of Venus,
Read your poems of fame,
Whilst daydreaming of fortune,
Underneath the planets and stars,
Let love serenade you,
Thy Valentine Queen,
In the gardens of paradise,
Let angels walk with you,
With bright wings of gold,
In beauty's light,
With songs and praise,
With beautiful birds singing,
As you enter the city gates of Rome,
Upon your war chariot,
A million laurels are thrown,
For you are a victorious glorious queen.

James Stephen Cameron

MY HEART DOES SING

My heart does sing,
Like the sweetest spring's song thrush
When you are around,
For then and only then, companioned,
True love is surely found.

Keith Newing

Valentine

Valentine,
Roses and wine.
An evening together,
. . . . so divine.

A candlelit dinner,
just for us two.
A perfect moment,
to say,
I love you.

Kevin Crookes

Inspired By Auden

Does it creep up on you
When you're not paying attention?
Is it bold when it turns up
Or is it full of apprehension?
Will you know it when you see it
Or is it something you must learn?
Is it really all around us
Or does it visit us in turn?
Does it fit into our lifestyle
Or is it something we should mould?
Do we know what we should do with it
Or do we need to be told?
Is it an inconvenience
Or a blessing in disguise?
Can we touch it with our fingers,
Can we see it with our eyes?
Does it come in manageable doses,
Or is it sometimes a little too much?
Is it a vicious slap across the face
Or a gentle, loving touch?
Is it as violent as a lion
Or as delicate as a dove?
Can someone, anyone tell me,
What's the story with love?

Charlotte Barnes

It Was Good To Be Living Then

The clock wakes up with
morning news.
the day is frosty, almost
bright. You doze on while
I make breakfast. One bird sings
for his morning crumb.
Load the car for a weekend stay,
Only car on the motorway,
Listening to the radio.
Sun comes up on the frosty
country roads, until
we reach the cottage where we'll stay.
My mum makes breakfast again.
But that was a long
long time ago. It was good
to be living then

The clock woke me up
with the news.
The day is frosty almost
bright. I make breakfast
for my dog and me
Lone bird sings for his morning
crumb. Get in the car
and drive away I miss you
on the motorway.
Your comments on the radio
Low sun glares off the shiny
A class road
I reach the home where my mum
waits to die, give her
gifts, show her my dog,
Talk about that time long long
ago. It was good,
it was, to be living then.

Fred Brown

Goodbye To Love

Was it only yesterday that this young woman disrupted my world?
Bringing a joy of life to all around her,
With her infectious smile and sparkling eyes.
Over time our friendship blossomed,
From moments together and shared laughter an affection grew.
Now her face is the last thing I see in my mind before I go to sleep.
And her name is on my lips as I awaken.
I hear her voice in the wind that gently blows through the trees,
And her laughter is the spring rain that caresses the leaves.
My only regret is that I will never again
Feel the warmth of her breath on my cheek as we sleep,
Or feel the softness of her breast against my skin.
For ours was a forbidden love,
That for now must remain hidden in winter's shadow.
But I know we will be together some day,
If not in this world then as moonbeams that dance across the night sky.

Stephen Mortlock

Romance

Romance is a gossamer thread
strung with diamond dewdrops.
It's moonlight and roses,
hearts and flowers,
holding hands and 'our song',
candlelit meals and lover's knots.

That gossamer thread will break
in sinks full of dirty crocks,
clothes on the floor,
sport versus drama and docs.

But sometimes from the charred remains
the phoenix of love will appear
like hope from Pandora's box.

Jackie Hinden

To Believe

To walk with her barefooted in the dew
To see a sunrise erupt from the gloom
To watch the moon as it takes the night
To see stars in her eyes a shimmering sight
To hold her hand in spite of the rain
To understand the diversion eked from pain
To want to be as to not be apart
To etch a future from an overgrown past
To desire this touch above all else
To give all life for her above the self
To wander only to find solace in she
To know forever would still too soon be
To believe as two that one is to live
To above all others only her to receive
To hold her heart as she holds yours
Is to believe your love will eternally soar
To walk barefooted in the dew.

Jade Smith

Aspects Of Love

When young we go to dance,
Being certain we look smart,
We waltz, quickstep and prance,
Hoping romance will start.

We still love to dance when mature,
For as long as our feet still work,
We don't have as much allure,
But I can enjoy a meal and a talk.

When love is yours in middle age,
He is your 'wrinkly Romeo',
With joy you become his wife,
He gives you a special glow.

Love has many attractions,
Whether youthful or mature,
It brings both pain and happiness,
But life needs love for sure.

Doreen Carne

DANCING WITH DR STONEFINGER

do you remember how we danced?
we pranced through the door
heading in unison
toward the dance floor
and as our eyes locked
as our bodies began to sway
everybody else just got out of the way

do you remember how we danced?
unmindful of how others glanced
youthful bodies in perfect sync
our hearts and souls were melded
we never had to think
and you would always grin at me
before you'd spin me

I remember how we danced
I remember the feeling
of being totally entranced
the universe
was ours to own
but you went away
and now I dance alone.

Kathy Patton McLemore

THE LAST WALTZ

Ahh, those were the good old days
With lights down low
Slowly waltzing round
A polished, ballroom floor
To dreamy music
Softly played
Spotlights trained
Upon a slowly turning crystal ball
Throwing countless coloured
Spots of light
Circling round the darkened room
While closely held within your arms
The one you love
Ahh.

George R Bell

L'Amour Lammermuir

Lovelier more, you're like Lammermuir Hills,
Flashing your flanks under hot harvest sun;
Beckoning me up through your golden grained fields,
Where breezes are rippling and cloud shadows run.
I eagerly follow your butterfly pathways
To bring me those breathtaking views of your moors:
Their heights stretching out to the purple cloud mountains.
Their flaunting of crags and of well-rounded laws.
Tease me half-sheltered in brochs tumble-broken,
Self-piteously tricked by your mood-swings to mist:
Or maroon me on banks where burn waters betoken
(Swirling peat brown, flashing silver with fish)
The depths I can't fathom of your female mind.
Inveigle me down the long cleughs to your valleys,
Beguile me beside a still loch where I find
That evening sky in your waters bring solace
To me in my peel tower crumbling through time.

Robert Newton

His Funeral

We gather glumly under trees,
Singly, or grouped in twos and threes,
Where drizzle and the dripping leaves
Anoint those whom his death bereaves.

Foretold as ticking of the clock,
Death, nevertheless, comes a shock.
I hear someone mumble his name
- To ask forgiveness, rue or blame?

Aware that high above, a jet
Blithely pollutes the place we're met,
Whilst mindless mower drones in waves
Among the stones that mark the graves.

It seems appropriate to say
Some words before we walk away.
But words won't come, and mourners go,
What's left to say? Best not to know . . .

Tony Newman

Burning In The Orange

A wisp of smoke escaped under the door,
So small in comparison to what would be inside,
But it caught the eyes of many,
Enough to raise an alarm,
And the mother was grateful,
For her precious son was trapped in the fire,
Choking to death by the suffocating fumes.

'My son! My son!' she called, despair in every word,
Her cries sent people plunging into the cloud of smoke,
Where they always came back empty-handed.
A guilty expression upon their faces,
For they had their children safe,
But she only had eyes for her son,
That searched everywhere but also came up empty.

Her tears were seen by all,
But every drop was a prayer for her son,
She ignored their words and their pity.
For she had not lost hope,
But they seemed so sure that he was gone,
That she found it rather difficult,
So she ran into the house, after the only person she loved.

People screamed for her to get out,
They called the rescuers,
She turned it out because she didn't understand,
How could her son slip from her grasp so easily?
He was there just a moment ago,
Entwining his tiny fingers with her dirty ones,
Where they stood together enjoying the company.

Too soon were there strangers,
Yanking her back, further from her son,
Away into the blackened night,
Where all was quiet now because people had given up,
But not her, she kept on wishing,
Glowing orange embers clung to her filthy soot-covered dress,
But she didn't care how she looked.

Her crazed expression was horrific to see,
For she knew what had happened,
They sprayed water, cooling everything down,
But showering her with wetness that she mistook for tears,
That shimmered on her cheeks from the fading flames,
Flames that died out long after her son did,
But she always prayed for him, even when she saw the dead eyes,
The limp body, his lifeless soul.

Lucy Edwards (15)

TENDER IS HIS LOVE

He mops her fevered brow
although she feels cooler now.
He hopes it soothes her.
He cannot say.

He strokes her lightly on the cheek
but she is so tired and weak
he doubts it comforts her.
It is his way.

Tender is his love for this woman
who has shared his life and still can
make his heart stop with fear
of losing her.

Timid is his smile of love
as his hand feels her hand move
closer so that they may
join together.

A tear of salty sweetness
alights on her palm like a kiss
as he senses the softness
of her last touch.

Denise Jarrett

SEA-COMBER

Eyes like jewels wash grey over blue.
As an ocean builds between us and
Your eyes are the waves that crash
Down upon me. You search my depths
For a gem, hidden in the murky deep.

But I stay on the craggy rocks,
Keeping myself. Holding me in, but my
Mind spills over. I am pouring myself into you.
I never wanted you. Sea comber;
A dumb creator of a world I can't endure.

Now the vast blue will roll on forever after
We are gone. Others will sail these waters
And hear our echoes over the moon's tide.
Hushing them asleep with our old song.
We were, we were, we were.

Matthew Fitzsimmons

WHAT IS THIS THING CALLED LOVE?

Though love's a thing of many splendours
Some negative emotions it engenders.
The wary and the faint of heart
Had best stay clear of Cupid's dart.
Don't put yourself in the situation
Of unreturned infatuation,
Lest jealousy rear its ugly head
And words of love remain unsaid.
Don't waste your time in amorous care
The perfect mate is waiting there.
Just sit tight – that's what to do –
There's someone searching just for you!

Lynn Widdows

LOVE AND PAIN

Love and pain placed a bet on the night we
lay together, each staking that they could
be the first dawn would bring. For bad or good
they chanced on senses, what we were to see,
smell, touch, taste and hear, and if we would be
sated by sensations. Misunderstood
or mesmerized: their stake asked if we would
favour a fixture we did not foresee . . .

The victor remains unclear, as we lay
like players still contending, bound by odds
where none is certain to win or lose.
Yet, considering the risks of yesterday
and raw emotions that play us like gods,
I am sure who I want to win the bet . . .

Samuel Saleem Fisher

WHO'S LOVE IS THIS?

Is this love mine?
Is this love yours?
I may know that I love you.
You may know that you love me.
But who is loving whom?

When, in rapturous union, the insight dawns
That there is really only one
Then I am also you
And you are also me,
Have always been
And always will be.

One in love
And being each the other,
We are this one
And this one is love.
So is this one everything that is?

William Weavings

WHAT IS LOVE?

Love . . .
What is love?

Love's that thing
That you can't quite see
But you know it's there
Because it's hit you
Like a shooting star

What is love?
Love is that wonder,
that sense of amazement
That time,
That space
It fills you up
And empties you

What is love?
The song you sing
The thought you had,
The ring you wear
Or the look you have
It brings you here
And takes you there again
Makes you whole
And tears you up.

This is love:
A something
A Someone
An eternity
A minute
A need
And a gift
From you
to The One

This is love.

Tiffany Aubrey

A Story Of Love

The love in your eyes
Frightens me,
Looks like the dark love
In the eyes of a moth.

Specially,
It frightens me
To fall in love.

Your love carves greedy
In my chest, in your chest,
In everyone's chest
Like a moth
As if our hearts are fed
With silky illusions.

You have the eyes of a moth.

Look at me
Carve from my soul
Carve from my soft, warm,
Woolen whispers.

Love me, riddle me,
Let's fall in love.

Let's raise together to the clouds
Me –
A frayed silky cloth
Of illusion, and you –
A greedy for love
Moth.

Doina Postolachi

Perfect

I wonder why certain people spend their whole lives looking,
Striving for the one ideal partner, - they can never have.
Deep belief in soulmates leads continually onwards,
Dismissing who happens to be in front of their noses,
Rarely a few lucky ones find their perfect partner,
Others continue looking hoping that one will be found.

Susan Mullinger

HANDS

Right now I'm missing his hands in mine,
Contemplating his fingers entwined,
We're truly a wholesome one, of a separate kind,
With our souls synthesised.
Yours; rugged and hard lined,
In the depths of a soft bind,
Engaged are our minds,
In a world full of wonderful and complicated signs.
Obviously our sentiment will shine,
Like the silk from a thread, so tender, so fine,
My thoughts inclined by you, occupied,
Will I ever be free of this fascinating rapture, I sigh.
Cos it's worth more than a dime, Ond; that's us,
This encounter between us rejoices in the essence of trust,
Our acquaintance, call it anything but lust,
Acknowledging it as an enticing entity is a must.
Refraining comparison to just another beau,
Defeating opinions of treacherous foes,
Your pure intentions that only I know,
Make a stunning complexion for a tasteful close.
Hence I salute your hands with an amorous smile.
They were the part of you held out to me while,
Tears poured and I tasted bile,
So when such pains occur again, I will hold them close when you're away many miles.

Nasima Begum

LOVE

The heart of human race is deceitful and desperately wicked;
Where man, woman, child slander, kill, swear and forget love
Where God's angels and cherubs that surround us are pained.

God's red heart beats with agape that no one fathoms.
For our lives of today and tomorrow he gave his.
On the Cross, His message to us – 'It is finished.'

We should try to be as much like Jesus Christ.
God's love for us translates into charity, kindness and patience.
Man, woman, child, sit, wine and dine, talk and laugh.

Kumbi Johnson

Don't Take Me Easy

Don't take me easy I'm a bird
For sacred singing once a year
Without sense and any fear
Like silver pipe you've never heard.

Don't take me easy I'm a snake
For lovely creeping in your soul
To change your heart to burning coal
And every day to crazy shake.

The harmony is rather rough,
Extremes make heart be so busy,
I wish you took them very easy,
Don't take me easy I'm your love!

Natalia Gorodova

Living Without You

The tongue unrolled
Speaking of what would numb the atmosphere
It repeated again,
The piercing phrase
The one in which, you hid in daze.
I miscalculated everything,
The emotions swirled out of my control
They were so chaotic, I could not patrol,
And now,
Here we stand,
We walk past each other as if we never exchanged words.
We stun our existence,
Connection,
Failed.
For me it is pride,
What is it for you?
I am patiently waiting, for those words that cross teeth and jump lips.
Before words came with ease . . .
Now they are forever my hurt.
If I had the words to let you know how much I miss you,
Would we reconnect?

Thandiwe Tafireyi

TOGETHER

Your cuddles, your touch, I love it so much,
Your kiss on my lips, makes my heart skip.
Your hand in mine, it feels so divine,
Your strength so strong, it can't be wrong,
Your love for me came slowly
Your passion's divine and it all feels just fine.
Your warmth against my body makes me go wobbly.
Your face so handsome, I'd pay any ransom.
You're smart and clever, let's live together.
You're sweet and kind, let's go unwind.
You're a joy to be with, so let's go and live
Together, together and stay forever, close so close
Until the end of time.

Julie Gibbon

HEARTLESS, SOULLESS

You are the light breeze meandering the highlands,
Flick the leaves into a spiral,
Entrance me.

You whip a fire into ragged sparks,
Direct the purge of the flames
And watch as they die.

You are the last scream,
The cry of the mourning sigil,
With me always.

Whip to the storm,
Black clouds,
The playful smile.

You brush the hair back from my face,
Twist a dangling lock,
Caress.

Eilidh Fergusson

Wedding – 9/9/09

The ring that unites us is complete:
the beginning is swallowed by the end,
creating a symmetry where odds and evens
are one, pivoting and turning both ways,
confusing the creature with creator
in a wild Celtic goose chase.

From this day on you are my alpha and omega;
a perfect balance of light and night in an equinox;
together we are the conjoined halves
of a Valentine heart.

May the hope of the present
spell the promise of tomorrow,
like the January head
on the stem of an amaryllis.

Do geese see God
on this palindromic day?

Frances Robson

Love

What does love mean?
Is it keeping him clean?
Is it washing and ironing,
And picking up his clothes?
Getting him up in the morning
Not letting him pick his nose?
Lying in bed in a rage
While he's fast asleep and snoring
Or listening to long winded tales,
Even though they're awfully boring
Yes love is all of this,
A compromise each day,
But I really must be honest,
I would have it no other way.

Sara Baker

I Think Of You

I think of you in the quiet moments
In the stillness of night
Upon a windswept hill
In an empty room
When the only sound is a ticking clock
I think of you now and again
When I can hear my own heart beating
Warm and safe, tucked up in bed
Dreaming of times long ago
When we walked together
With laughter ringing in our ears
My thoughts of you are triggered
By little things
The wind that rustles amongst the leaves
Rainbows we watched slowly fade
Your zest for life, your tender heart
I hope that sometimes you remember me
When a rainbow fills the sky
I walked in paradise once
But now am left upon an ocean
Staring at the setting sun
To be engulfed in pitch-black emptiness
But I know the morning will bring the light
And I will walk upon new shores
With faded memories
Almost forgotten
Except for the sound of a ticking clock.

David M Walford

To Be In Love

To be in love
Is like catching lightning
The darkness inside disappears
You see the world through a new dimension
The clouds are pink and
The sea is red.

Suddenly you feel what he feels too
He crawls under a rock
But you know that love is not a one way street
As it runs both ways.
And you'll go through the sun and the showers to get to him.

His accidental touch makes jelly of you
And your heart flushes with weakness
You cannot gaze in his eyes
'Because your pulse must not say
What must not be said.'

When he is not there
Your soul loses its shape
And your heart begins to stall
There is no escape.

The love you rode the waves for
Was never meant to last
It lies at the bottom of the ocean
A rusting wreck.

Rujina Akther

OUR 8TH ANNIVERSARY

It was mine and Rae's Anniversary yesterday
And I got thinking about how we met
We both went on our mobiles one day
And logged into the Internet
We went into a thing called Genie Chat
. . . which was taken over by o2
We chatted about this and that
And spoke to other folk too
Rae was in a hospital bed
Away up in Lossiemouth
He was knocked off his lorry he said
And he actually lived down south
We spoke to each other online only
We knew we had to be aware
Rae's username suggested he was lonely
But our times online were rare
Soon we would arrange a time
To try and get on to chat
We weren't committing any crime
So we shared our welcome mat
We hit it off right from the start
Chatting and laughing now and again
And although he was taking over my heart
We agreed we'd like to stay friends
Then our email addresses were exchanged
And we kept in touch when we could
Then a trip home for Rae was arranged
And it hurt like I knew it would
Our mobile numbers were exchanged next
He was in a helicopter going to Dorset
I waited and waited for a text
But my wishes weren't met
Then much later on that night
My phone rang and it was Rae
He called to say he was alright
But he was 500 miles away
He said he'd like to keep in touch
I was his 'wee angel' he said
I liked him very, very much
And wished he was with me instead
When Rae's injuries had all been mended
He asked if he could come to see me
To thank me was what he had intended

But that didn't work out you see
All these words about just being friends
Had went slightly out of control
He went back down south again
But to come back up was is goal
We visited each other for a year
Our friendship grew into love pretty fast
We always wanted each other near
But didn't know if our love would last
After that year of visits had passed
We decided that Rae would move in
Together we would be at last
And nothing could hide my grin
A year of living together went by
I wasn't prepared for what came next
Rae done something that made me cry
He proposed to me by text
So now we've been married for 8 years
Though we've had our ups and downs
There's been laughter, and some tears
And even several frowns
But it shows you what can be done
If you take things slowly you see
We've had more than our share of fun
And Rae's angel, I hope, I'll always be . . .

Lynda Johns

ANYTHING . . .

You may know this . . . perhaps not,
But I think I'll say it anyway.
You mean a lot to me,
What you do is certainly your choice,
But remember,
I never asked you to do anything.
I don't want you to do anything,
I love you.
It doesn't matter if you believe me or not,
Just don't try to change anything.
The way things were, let them return to being that way.
Without you in it,
Life doesn't mean anything.
Whatever the reason behind it, I don't care,
If you go back to being who you were,
I won't ask anything.
You can't change what you are for me.
In time perhaps you'll realize,
That what you're doing, hurts so much
And in the end it won't come to anything,
Because you are, what you are to me,
That will never change.
I love you
And I need to know . . . I mean something to you . . . anything . . .

Ghazal Choudhary

UNTITLED

Pretty is a word I would use
If there was word I was forced to choose
To describe you to a passer-by
To say you're not amazing would be a lie.

Beautiful face framed with flowing curls
That when you're thinking, you like to twirl.
Elegant air paired with a cheeky smile,
Make me laugh all the while.

Ryan Manning

UNTITLED

Do you know what love is, Mother, do you know?
And can you tell me how to find it, where to go,
How I'll know it if I find it, does it show?
Oh, do you know what love is, Mother, do you know?

Daughter, love has many faces, you will see.
Just think how I love you and you love me
And how we love your father both and then how he
Loves us and you will know what love is, do you see?

Is that the whole of love then, Mother, nothing more?
What if tall young men come calling at the door?
What if someone says he loves me? Is he sure
Of what he says or just pretending, nothing more?

Two things you need to know, my child, only two –
If what he says to you is really true
And then, if you love him, how much he means to you –
But oh, if there is nothing you can do.

But if we loved each other, what could interfere?
Belonging to each other year by year
Our love would be too strong for us to fear
That anything could part us, surely that is clear.

Love is not so simple, child, as you may find
If love as passion conflicts with love that's kind,
If your heart's yearning still cannot be blind
To how you'd hurt the loved ones that you'd leave behind.

Now I don't understand you, Mother, do you mean
That love can cause you pain, can intervene
In happiness – has that ever been?
Mother, is that a sort of love that you have seen?

Yes, I know what love is, darling, how I know,
Breaking my heart to love him yet to let him go –
Quickly, come here and kiss me, dear, and let me show
How much I love you. There. Now off you go.

Michael Robertson

ANGEL UPON A CLOUD

Fragmented emotions apocalyptic within my heart
Every decision a tidal wave of events to follow
I climb high for air of which to breathe
Stifled, I begin to slip back to Earth
Dizzy with a thousand unanswered questions
Confused for what direction to take next
I sit alone and ponder my uncertainty
Dazed by a multitude of dilemmas
Clouded by a mountain of doubt
I close my eyes
Through the darkness my dream comes alive
Taking form from the depths of my imagination
Resurrecting the aspirations of my faith
Guiding my soul to what I seek
I spot my vision
An angel sat upon her cloud
Wings open, ready to fly
To soar the cosmos
Spreading warmth wherever she goes
I open my arms in anticipation
Hopeful, I will catch her when she falls
To hold her close to my skin
Our embrace an everlasting moment to savour
Interlocked with the intensity of two lovers
Sweet music echoes all around
As our bodies melt into one
Forging a world we can share forever
Overwhelmed in love, I smile with satisfaction
Filling my entirety with confidence we will always be
Comfortable, I open my eyes
Night turns to day
Transcending all thoughts from view
Expelling my vision
Melting the dream I hold so dear
Sending my angel back to her cloud within my mind.

Lee Hunt

This Barren Land

Hymns Pantycelyn froze upon my breath
one evening in that dark and dismal place,
the Baptist Chapel pew, as cold as death,
the Valley's sadness etched upon your face.
But as Moriah's preacher ranted wild
you looked at me and smiled,
           I was beguiled.

We loosed the shackles of that godly crowd,
we laughed and lied beneath the Gower rain,
we blasphemed, teased and taunted, wrangled, rowed,
we loved and cried and cried and loved again.
Now as the Rheidol waters tumble by
I think of you and sigh –
           And wonder why.

Peter Davies

The Balladry Of Damaged Hearts

Madeleine Peyroux brings
A most intimate style
With Gauloise elements:
They're much in evidence,
When two lovers just can't reconcile.

In the balladry of damaged hearts,
There is often one who's been untrue,
And obtained wrong amounts of delight –
While his lady-love mourns through the night
That should have been their rendezvous.

Nicole's wicked cad lover
Leaves her in the stocks
For malevolent neighbourhood scorn.
What did she hope for – future love sworn?
Her emotions were his shuttlecocks.

Gillian Fisher

Making Senses

Seeing is still too hard
It breeds touching.

Eating was once easy
When mouths strayed, where love crept to hollow.

Smelling was an oligarchy
Circling the omphalos
Of our civet state.

Feeling was a sweet freedom
Sliding naked through the warm emulsion of breath.

Now,
Looking into eyes that once loved you to sleep
You are lulled into the slink of belonging.

Gazing into smoky azure depths,
Betrayed into retrieving the pearls of an ancient bond.

But surface cautiously
This is enemy territory.

Retreat,
Step over the shards of our buried love
And walk towards knowing.

Suzanne Stevenson

Heart Beat

If it gets any wider,
The breath of my smile will tickle my ears
As I stand,
On frozen ground, the sky has fallen
You're such a beautiful sound.
Send me a stiff breeze as I wish
I could fall into your arms.
Horn on heart.
I swear your love is weightless,
So I carry it with me everywhere.
Always, in my pocket, in my mind
There's no wrong to your rights.
Faultless.

Rasharda Thompson

THE REAL THING

'Did my heart love till now?'
Or did it wait, like Henry's for the Real Thing,
The one that knocks and says: 'Accept me, here I Am?'

Or did it make false idols out of fear?
To be a virgin in her twenties,
To smile a crooked smile when someone mentions sex?

Or did it grasp at sparkles, shooting bright,
Illuminating night sky, but –
Elusive, and illusory?

It's different now. For he who owns my heart
Is true. First – to himself, then to his path, then me.
From this, all other virtues flow and hold me.

And now my heart is tended to, and fed, at home,
All doors and windows open, it feels right.
'For I ne'er saw true beauty till this night.'

Oxana Poberejnaia

MY WORLD

My family are my world
I'm the luckiest girl alive
My darling, loving husband
My beautiful children and I

Whatever the weather
Whatever the storm
Whatever the joy
Whatever life can throw at us

We face it altogether
We face it as a family
We face it as a one
We face it as a team

Our family is strong
It's us against the world
Life will never break us
Because we have each other

I'm the luckiest girl alive
To have a family like mine.

Carena Mills

Pining For Her Soul

Pining for a soul
Who lives many miles
Away. I worry
Wish I didn't have to
Wish she were with me
Here where nature loves
With open arms in
The cradle of summer
Her eyes from afar
Make me act honest
I resolve to be
Better at loving
I want to be near
Where her lungs breathe life
Her tread makes dust fly
And her words look large.

Muhammad Khurram Salim

Patricia

I hold your face in my hands,
And brush away the hair from your eyes,
As we stand alone, in a crowded street,
Watching the world around us collapse,
We can smile, knowing if nothing else,
Our love will survive.
I've travelled the Earth to find you,
And many moons have passed,
You are the one that's meant for me,
The first I've loved,
And the last.
Everything I do,
Is just a means to an end,
To stand beside you for the rest of time,
To be the one, you always run to,
As your lover, and your friend.

Dale Alun Duggan

This Day

When we look back
From the years to come
Will we remember
Was there rain or sun?

And will we recall
All the names and faces
Or will memory fade
Leaving vague, happy traces?

We might forget the music
The tearful, smiling sighs
But always we'll remember
The love in each other's eyes

So if all that remains
Of this day is me and you
Then that's enough
To last our whole life through

For one thing we'll know
Forever and a day
The two of us were there
That's all we need to say.

Carolyn Fittall

Love Muffin

Just when I had given up hope of happiness
A man with an irresistible smile walked into my life
Mesmerizing me with good looks, ruggedness and charm
Eyes that transfix my gaze making me smile
Sending a stream of sensations through my body which tell me he is the one!

Getting kissed by him gives me warm tingles
Relaxing on my bed embraced in his arms makes me so contented
I have never met someone so quirky, so understanding, so generous
For all my worries that hold me back he helps me solve them, he helps me change
Fun and adventure is guaranteed, I have a new zest for life
I want to make him happy, to share my life with him, to give him all that I am
No one can compare to my joy, my love. James Griffin.

Sarah George

THE FABRIC BORN

I know well that feeling,
For hate to turn to love and love to hate,
Make no mistake that I am reeling
And I would not forgive, but I would take.

Two sides of the same coin, air and ether,
I'm so high and drunk, I can't relieve,
This dreadful feeling I am feeling,
I cannot hope to just give in, to just believe.

Why are you so far away?
Why make such a mockery of me?
Why do I turn nothing into something?
Why can't I just be what I can be?

Mother may I? May I?
The rot has rotted through all it can,
And I have spoken words meaning nothing,
And I have walked these barren lands.

I have walked these barren lands, these city seascapes,
Yes I have walked to the end of every pier.
I have walked where you've been lying,
I've walked this way for a thousand years.

A sudden change in tide, I do return,
To turbulent sea from which I'm torn,
But more than that I am merely other,
Than the fabric less stirred, the fabric born.

The unbecoming world in all its glory
In all its terror, in everything it has to tell
I have heard each beautiful, awful story
I have scaled each high, and plumbed each well.

I've been to the depths, don't think I haven't,
I've sold every horror you can sell,
I've sold it all and dressed it up as something,
That Adam would perceive before he fell.

And Eve would eat the apple boldly,
And Lilith in the wings would nod her head,
For she would know it's merely an illusion
That Eden is only a dream for restless dead.

I've scaled the heights, don't think I haven't,
I've conquered that which isn't conquerable at all,
When 'impossible' has no meaning,
You can do anything, and do it all.

Yes, I know too well that feeling, when
Hate turns to love, and love to hate.
I know too well it leaves me reeling,
I know it all too well, make no mistake.

Aleksandra Petrova

Pretty Woman

I went on holiday to Florida,
Met a man – young enough to be my son,
I needed a ride, he was my chauffeur,
I became a star in 'Pretty Woman'.

He drove the limo' – I sat at the rear
He – tall dark and handsome, with a great smile
Guess what I called him – 'My young Richard Gere'
I was 'Julie Roberts' – mile after mile.

We shopped at thrift shops and the fancy mall:
Bought clothing and food and diet coke too.
Lampshades and paintings, he helped with them all
Tell me – has this ever happened to you?

He drove me to the airport, London bound
A bear-hug and a smile: a great way to say 'Goodbye'
A missed beat in my heart – what's this I found?
Joy! Was that really a tear in my eye?

We had much fun 'hanging out together'
Smiles, jokes and laughs: some of the best ever!

Prof Mary May Robertson

Parts Of Ourselves

Parts of ourselves
We give away
To anyone

And no one wants it
When we need to
Give the most
Important part
Of our heart

We lose it
Most often.

Piotr Gabryelski

You Know I Lust You

I love y . .
Hello, excuse me, can I stop you there
Sorry to interrupt this most intimate affair.
I couldn't but notice the words about to be said
And thought, a quick pause perhaps might be needed instead
I hear it quite often, the pouring of one's heart
But it's easily dispersed like a wind carries fart
It's true, talk is cheap
And a heartache you'll reap
Consider your next words
'Cause lust can be a curse.

It's a temporary fixation
A moment of elation
But love is forever
The two sewn together
For that, are you ready?
If not, take it steady.

Tony Kangah

Let Me In

Have faith in me, I won't run away
This I promise you today.

I have to confess
Sometimes I feel like I don't know you
I wanna know you
I wanna feel you
Open up to me
And let me in

I know you find it hard to let me in
I know you're scared to let me in
You're like two people at once
One day you're full of love
Next day you're full of hate
Am accepting you as you are
Baby don't push me away.

You can trust me
You can rely on me
I promise I won't run
I promise I'll be there
You say you're fearless
You say you're strong
You say a lot of things,
How can I know this if you never let me in?

I know you find it hard to let me in
I know you're scared to let me in
You're like two people at once
One day you're full of love
Next day you're full of hate
Am accepting you as you are
Baby don't push me away.

Adwoa Asiedu

How Love Lives

It's an odd thing
Love
Lives like it's on its own, owns not belonging to
The heart.

Torn from time's wing
It flies with senseless freedom
Fills gaps with swiftness: forgetting, forgetting
Feeds moments with rashness; upsetting, upsetting.

Skilful, like an art
As it feeds through the clock's cracks
Into the body, breaking off the hands
To us you're helpless, you're strung in love's strand.

On its terms now
It's the only way
It will take everything from your grasp, consume you with its past,
But let you go at last with your battered heart, unmasked.

Leave it, don't touch – it needs no other force to do its deed.
It has hope
It has no queue,
It captures souls
It captured you.

Saba Ikhlas Malik

Untitled

Your mind is like a crossword
All what you say isn't heard
I sit and try and figure you out
But all the while I am filled with doubt
That I could get the answer wrong
But I have been here for so, so long
Trying to figure out the why it doesn't quite fit
And where and why this addiction first hit
But I'll carry on solving this
In the back of my mind
In the hope that like me
You won't leave this riddle behind.

Ellis Elliott

A Special Day

V ibes which were hidden deep inside our souls,
A re finally emerging now to reach their target,
L ove letters, candid poems and red roses,
E mulate without fear, right across the poles.
N othing will stop the sweet, yet astute Eros,
T o thrust his little arrows in true hearts,
I nitiating the foundations of destined unions,
N udging lost lovers, so their paths can cross.
E njoy the feeling this wonderful day brings,

D ance through the night to silent music.
A mass the mesmerizing spell that's set to heel,
Y ears of beatitude and everlasting springs.

Demetra Ciobanu

Lilia By The Fountains

A wash of white feather
The swan sweeps to where the water
Breaks, her weight.

The black smack of velvet
Glass ripples the ice jacket
Six tears strip the melting surface
Six more pass the floating world.

I shine soft, I am the moonlight
I burn beams to her cold skin
Lilia dries by the fountains, panting
Untying the stillness of the statues.

The midnight swimmer sculls
The pink reeds kiss, the bank staunches
The sun calls, my eye shatters.

Charles Baylis

LIFE LINES

I touch the creases of her cheeks as they rise,
the same smile, like the crescent of a honey summer moon
below her beauty spot, multiplied as moles
counting the years of our union

From our first winter together,
we walked amongst the dead
leaves, trees left bare like the broken children
of our new neighbour's homes

and on our return, removing your gloves
to feel the softness of your skin,
I traced your lifeline
to this very day.

Carmina Masoliver

A LETTER HOME: PORT ARTHUR, TASMANIA

Your skin daubs
My fingers, syllables,
surveying your body's punctuation.

As knee prefixes thigh,
head suffixes chest
I meander through ridged commas;
ephemeral question marks.

Your body's punctuation endures
Like the Tasmanian doglines.

So, stretching
across Mt Wellington
and the Atlantic,
I kiss a full-stop.

Stephen Foot

LOVE

Love shouldn't be for rent
Brought in minutes and in hours,
Love shouldn't be left to die
Like that of cut flowers.
Love shouldn't hold no distance
For one heart to ache in pain,
Love should be free to fly
Not weighted down in chains.
Love shouldn't hold a price tag
For love they say is free,
It shouldn't keep you prisoner
When love holds the key.
Love has no boundaries
To reach every given soul,
It plays without an orchestra
Where gentle music flows.
Between the hearts of lovers
Every note rehearsed,
To the tune of, 'I love you'
Found in every verse.
Love is something we find
And sometimes we sadly lose,
Bringing heartache and pain
When it makes us choose,
From what is right or wrong
Or fated not to be,
But love will always guide us
To our destiny.
Hearts are like jigsaw puzzles
They beat with one missing piece,
Until we find our true love
And then our heart's complete.

Lisa Jane Mills

Aspects Of Love

Life as it used to be. Remembering a tramp of long ago who would not hurt a fly. This is my dedication to him although long gone.

A tramp of old
Bearing his soul
To the world outside living bold
The natural world his only friend
Where nature surrounds his sleeping trends,
Morning sees him on the move again
His secretive movements safely intact
Within a world of no turning back,
Secretly I envied his strength
Plodding along with no true intent
Changing scenery allowing contact
Accomplished beauty complete his tracks,
When troubled with aching feet
He finds a spot to retreat,
All he needs as a prize
Comfort in disguise
As a child all I wanted to do
Was request his life's views
You see in my childhood days
All fear was erased
From a gentle rugged old man
With nothing left of a clan.
Only the natural world to expand
Contented to live life as he planned.

I will remember him for the rest of my life.

Barbara R Lockwood

A Woman Of Beauty

A moment in time, captured, remembered with stirring felt
Across a crowded room, engaged with others drawn to you, heart did melt
Unaware that I was watching, attracted to, you were the one
A woman of beauty, held in time, knew reason theatre of life had come
Then you looked my way, caught my eye, a heart beat missed
I made my way through the gathering, hoping those lips I would kiss

A connection made, relationship confirmed, warm and close
Arrived at your side, enjoyed your company, desired it most
For me, no one else in that room, although it was crowded
You stood out in my mind, an impression which my desire grounded
Time has since passed, living together for many years hence
I would not have missed it, although early years were sometimes tense

We do still laugh, remembering the times, people we have known
A shared humour, pause and think, fabrics together stitched and sown
Each the tides turned by the moon, with the cycle constant and forever
As life's wheel turns its position, so destiny brings two people together
Can see through the haze, loudly says it was meant to be
Moments captured, shared, watching the surge of a crashing sea.

Your company I seek, to know you well is time well spent
You came into my life and changed it, as if you were sent
I still look for the bright joy that oozes from you
That it is directed and inclusive, this is what I am happy with too,
The seasons come and go, I hope in partnership, that time is kind to us
My love for you grows with each 'flight of the swallow' there is no rush.

Ron Constant

Isolated Thoughts

You hate it when I sit there quiet
Not saying anything
Often it must feel that I don't want to be there

Sometimes I wonder what I must have done in my life
To have your love
To be with you

Sometimes it dawns on me that I could wake up
This could be a dream
One day we might both end up on two sides of the world
Living a different life to what we are now
We may be happy we could be sad
We might choose to remember these days or choose not to

We might sit a million miles apart thinking where we both are
With all the dreams we had together
With all the fun we shared
Our future so uncertain

Sometimes I sit there quiet
Thinking of all the stories all the laughter
All the love

Sometimes I sit there quiet
Praying you'll be mine

Forever.

Saara Mahomed

Untitled

Shall I compare you to a summer's rose?
Though it's nothing on you I suppose.
Well then, I'll try a swan
But you're more like Teflon.
Not grey, but tough and strong.
My warrior princess,
Face so changeless.
My rock through all time,
And I'm glad you're mine.

Hayley Rowe

Birthing Poem

You were not exactly contorted
But pain was written there
Reaching for the gas and air
Pulling at your hair with both hands
Then circling the midwife's wrist
With fingers tight
'Oh God,' squeezed out of clenched teeth
And bending over
Then resting for a paused breath
'Can't I walk about?'

It's not a dignified business this birthing
But when Mrs Doubtfire saw your bum uncovered
She tutted, pulling sheet to hide what, who cares?
The trolley set
Internal done and plastic hook
Eyeing your unbroken waters.
Then it came
One deep wave that brought your child
To birth:
'Don't push, breathe, that's a girl!'

She kept on calling you Katheryne
'It's Kate.'
I didn't know what to do except stick close by you.
I wanted to wave a magic wand
To bring your own mother home
I wanted to shout at the midwife
To let you do it your way
But in the end you did.

From your living womb
Came the brightest light
A tiny screaming child
Reaching out to you
Both wanting to be held and hold

He came to you
Caressed, 'Hello tiny'
Your voice a singing song
Of mother's ancient melodies . . .
I left after a short while
For mother's rituals are private things
Rooted in the heart of Eve.

Von Corner

DEAR TREE

Fading tree
You appear so small
Or is it only the distance that separates?
As long as your piece of thread
Or my threadbare youth

Knowledgeable tree
So silent in the bustling madness
Of this life too short for no man
You have seen far more winters than star-crossed lovers
And perhaps he has wondered many times
Held aloft and kept safe in your strong boughs.

Brave tree
For you no chair or table top shall be sliced off your back
No candlesticks of wood nor tear-drenched letters
Or needles to knit the complexities we shroud ourselves in
No goblet overflowing with unrequited love
No.
You are worth far more

Subtle tree
I hear you watching me
Can he feel this – wherever he wanders
You are the compass uncarved
That no one even knows they are holding

Beautiful tree
The adjective no justice offers
Your earthy scent as bright and vibrant as any scarf or perfume
Your mismatched perfection too precise to imitate
And as he smiles your beauty further extends
And no boundaries exist
Regarding paradise

Sad tree
The secrets well concealed
In your entanglement of roots
Your high branches
Your infinity of leaves
You are life so bright so beautiful
But as always this is interwoven with deep sadness
And many stories etch themselves on your bark
Of loneliness
Of grief
Of the passionate love that you bring from one year to the next and on and on

Do you not grow weary?
Do you not feel fear?

Wise tree
You have seen far more than he or me
Than the women that gossip
And men that believe they lead our country
Than the young fools who fancy themselves as in love
And the brave soldiers that carry their honour into battle
Trusting man's instructions trusting man's decisions, perhaps even man's depiction of God

But who do you trust?
Do you trust the earth that beds our strong roots?
The sun that warms your body?
The spirit that brings you life from season to season year to year
That soars just above your highest branches
I see you reaching for it
As on tiptoe we do the same.

And if I could have one year
To spend beneath your limitless boughs
With the man I fancy myself to be in love with (for I am a young fool though so old and cynical in mind)
With afternoons spent reading some delight
And licking ice cream from my fingers
As the sun's delicate freshness tickles my face
And my love's sweet dark eyes nurse my soul
That would be my bliss, old tree.

Fruitful tree
Who feels far more than man and his possessions
Who gives for the pleasure of others
Without hesitation
You are always there
Whilst unconditional love is something that man cannot grasp
You paint the picture so plainly
So simply
And it is the most beautiful and haunting portrait of happiness and sadness
The two are one
As your leaves brightest green later burn to fiery copper
What a lot you have taught me
I am so thankful

So now, dear tree I will leave you
But I hope to meet again
One autumn day as your leaves are scattered
Like confetti on two young fools
I will smile and kiss and cry

And look up at the spot where I one day see another young girl
With her soul full of joy and love
Sit and listen to your conversations with the wind
And learn all about the sadness of humanity
Our brief time on this Earth which we spend fumbling around trying to work out where we are going
I trust you to be her compass
And I will love the moments that we will share with you
As she learns about the bliss that is all around us
That can be found if only you are willing to stop and open your eyes
I will see you there.

Sophie Revell

HEARTBREAK

For my heart is broken,
A life of misery has woken,
My heartbeat has stopped
A lonely life I must now adopt.

We were together for many a year
But lightning struck and spoilt the cheer,
We held hands and vowed to stay in touch
But I knew I couldn't expect much.

It was the moment I had dreaded
In conversation that break up was embedded,
Tears of heartbreak and memories of happiness, a dangerous concoction
Staying apart was the only viable option.

For now my life is a broken mirror
To trust a close one again sends a shiver,
A shiver down my spine and I cry and shake
For this is true heartbreak.

Ramandeep Kaur

Untitled

The exotic harmonious rhythms,
Of her warm and inviting waves.
The intuitive appreciation you have
As you immerse yourself in her
You crave . . .
More . . .
But still you are unsure
Of how deep you want to go
The point that you find yourself at now is
Comfortable but shallow . . .
Yet there is so much more to explore
But you're scared that you will drown
In the deepest part of this emotive ocean
Afraid you will never get out . . .

But once you go beneath the surface
You'll be amazed at what you see
Beauty running ever deep
All throughout her sea
Life resides within her
Serenity and peace,
Her current at times overwhelming and harsh
But she longs for understanding, respect and dignity.

Death also plays its part in this ocean
But you should fear it not,
For death means not the end this time
But a rebirth of the energies lost
It is:
Death of your lonely reality
Death of your stoic control
Death of your built up ego
But never ever the death of your soul . . .

Sherrie Molyneaux

That First Day

I never told you how much I loved you
And did from that first day.

I watched you walk across the road
I watched you walk away.

You walked inside my head that day
And lodged within my brain.

I knew I had to see you again
That to me was plain.

Everything I did and said
Was with you inside my head

Even when I sat to eat
Or took myself to bed

You were there inside my head
Waiting to be fed

You were there in the morning
When I looked into the mirror

I could not work, I could not see
Only think of you and me

I know that we will meet again
I feel it in my bones

If only you knew how I feel
And how my heart groans

My love for you is paramount
I'm a detective on a case

I will not rest till I have kissed
The lips upon your face.

Janet Vessey

H¹O

Just more water under the bridge
So I'll calmly wave
But one day the river will rage and rise
I will be touched and the gap passed
Lifted without force
Hooked without doubt
She will wash over and cleanse me
Leaving me flooded
No longer an island
Laden with stone
Drifting alone
Without ebb or flow or ever knowing
Then I will sink
Intoxicated
Filling myself
Breathing, in the currents that move me.

David Cameron

DISTANT LOVE

Seen you from a distance, I felt my heart skip,
I looked at you, just one small glance,
Your face in my mind, never to be forgotten.
Just a small courage and I can speak with you
Tell you my name.
And then my ideal fades as you hug another.
Your face never forgotten will scar me for a little while
Maybe one day our paths will cross and I can listen to your voice
Maybe one day it will be our best choice.

Mike Whaley

VILE DECEIT

You came to me through
Coercion and deceit
When our lips met
My eyes opened to
Our nakedness
And the world around us

Your bitter-sweet seduction
Carried us from the garden
Of paradise into the additive
Delights of the house of pain
Anguish, sadness and sorrow

A sorrow and sadness that harkens
Back to a love that was ever true and
Pure like the full moon rising resplendent
And voluptuous to light our garden of
Calm peaceful love
A love that is now a lost paradise

A paradise of innocence now lost
To our opium-filled days of pain, anguish
And fleeting passions, carried on the river
Of our mortality, to be dashed against
The rocks of disappointment, and our
Hearts shattered into shards of emotional
Splinters and sprinkled throughout time.

Now we cling to the flickering
Embers of hope, and labour
To ease the scarred emotions
Of our hearts, so as to keep
Love and hope alive, as the
Poppy of life give s no respite
Or access to the idyllic and
Tranquil garden of Shangri La

So we must toil daily in the
House of opium-filled pain and
Sorrow, to mend our broken hearts,
And ease our pain in moments of
Fleeting happiness, to promise
Ourselves that tomorrow will
Bring true love and happiness

Oh cruel love of deceit
Will our hearts never sing
Again in unison to the music
Of love's sweet melody
Will we never walk in
Harmonious happiness
Must our first kiss forever
Be a bitter bile of loss and sorrow.

Ezekiel Headley

Budding Roses

Where roses bloom
My darling bulbs of May.
Why settle in the ground and not grow?
When summer is so close.
Where you shall bloom?
So take shape for tomorrow your siblings will sprout
In a garden full of delightful plants
Your roses will shower us with divine colours
In so many fragile petals leaving me speechless on new arrivals
Only for show for our very eyes
The crop pops up in spring, summer and wintertime
The rose learns how to survive country life outside.
Its purpose is so romantic; a mark of respect for your Valentine
With one single rose we take it as a symbol of pleasure
Naturally to have and to hold
In our watchful gaze
Left on its throne in a special vase
In our home
As the summer unfolds, time elapses
The sun rises and falls
Even the daffodils appear to greet the rose
The rose grows in luxury and dwells with bluebells and poppies.
Where bees and butterflies play
Rain starts to shower the rose
The stalks are strong and the head fades
Left standing entwined in fertile soil
As the turf is replenished with the loving touch of the Gardeners' helping hands.
By cutting the flowers and watering them with gentle ease
Praying for another new year for rose bed flowering
Making another glorious picturesque scene in 2012.

Nassira Ouadi

Darling, I Love You

Maybe you can hold me close, never let me go
You are the one for me and that will always show
Make me smile make me cry, let the world go by
Lie in bed all day and you will see just why

That our time together is so great to me You bring out all the best attributes that I have in me
I can see that you care every touch, every kiss
When I'm not around you, you're the only one I miss.

Please don't ever go, I don't want to leave
Without you by my side then I will surely grieve
I will sit at home and sing our love song
You fill me up with courage and you make me strong.

And I know that my heart will not lie to me
It just sometimes paints the pictures I don't wanna see
But my heart knows that life is a storybook,
There's always a happy ending but I just can't look.

So just be my love each and every day,
I know that you will promise now but I want you to say
Those three little words that will make me smile
Tie my tummy up in knots and make my life worthwhile.

Love is such a tricky thing to describe but ignore
When all the things seem right then I just seem to want more
You can steal my heart you can take my words too
And whisper in my ear 'Darling, I love you.'

Steffi McIntyre

The Priceless Pearl

None pines for love so much as he
Who never loved at all.
None sells his soul but for a pearl
Deemed unobtainable.

So do I pine for one I knew,
But never made my own –
The priceless pearl whose loveless heart
Was chiselled out of stone.

Stephen Smith

PROTECTED HEART

Heart protected
Hidden and sheltered
Walls all around
Safe from destruction.

Feeling confusion
Barriers falling
Anxious and panic
Heart pounds inside me.

Emotions racing
Strange and fearful
Vulnerable, frightened
Exposed and so helpless.

Angry, self-punished
Sanity tortured
Fighting my feelings
Losing the battle.

Sandra McGowan

A WOMAN-CHILD'S YEARNINGS

Stars.
You can't count them. Too many. Too far away.
All the wishes and hopes and dreams.
Up, up, up.

If I had a bottle of glitter, I would pour it on the floor,
because I like glitter.
(All the glitters, aaaallll the glitters.
Like stars. In my room. And I can *touch!*)

Oh – touch! Touch me, or I will fade away. With your touch, I . . .
With your touch, I . . .
am me.
(I'm always me, you know.
But your helping hand helps.
Even a hard touch like a smack across the face would help me now.
Smack! Like that. Like the shocks to the heart in hospital)
Make me come alive! Quick, before the heart stops beating!

Eva Kaye

Aspects Of Love

Forty eight years ago,
Although we meant every word, when we took our vows,
We really had no understanding of what it entailed,
When promising to love, honour and obey,
To stick together through sickness and health,
For richer or for poorer and all manner of adversity.

Through these years
There have been many trials and tribulations, storms and tempest,
That could have blown us over and separated us,
A continuous fight over the children,
When they were naughty, how to punish them,
No time for us, or what we wanted,
When one was at work,
The other at home looking after them.

Arguing over the lack of money,
Grumbling when he spent it in the pub,
Feeling put out when he came home late,
And putting his dinner in the bin,
When it got cold or burnt.

Disappointed in him when he stood lovingly admiring some other woman,
Making me feel small and insignificant and shabbily dressed.

Working to change each other,
To become one person not two,
Fighting with each other all the way up to this point in time,
Then ill health finally brought us together,
We worked together, in factories for many years,

Finally going everywhere together,
Although now in our seventies,
We don't find much to talk about,
And certainly nothing more to argue over,
In the end we came to the conclusion that we would agree to disagree.

These days we talk more to our animals than to each other.
We don't even fight over what we are going to watch on TV.
I don't know if he feels as terrified as I do,
About when one of us is no longer here,
Feeling so vulnerable,
Tired of fighting battles alone.

We've got used to the other one being there at night, in the morning, all through the day,
After the forty eight years, I can honestly say I would do it all over again.
I still love him and he's my best friend, now and always my Valentine.

Josephine Smith

THE WEDDING DAY

The bride arrives in a horse-drawn carriage,
An ethereal vision of beauty in ivory silk and Brussels lace,
Her head crowned by a bouquet of lilies,
Happiness beams across her joyful face.
Church bells chime merrily from the steeple,
The best man, provides friendly support to the groom by his side,
Colourful hats compete for everyone's attention,
To a musical fanfare, here comes the lovely bride.
Vows are made as the rings are exchanged,
The happy couple declare their love for each other,
United in spiritual and legal connection,
They have no one else now, but one another.
The reception is a Heaven of red roses and white chocolate swans,
Women await the bridal bouquet with joyful celebration,
Tears of joy are shed by everyone all around,
Love and laughter fill the summer air with jubilation.
Speeches are made as the champagne flows,
The couple dance to the waltz on the marquee floor,
The wedding cake is cut to a round of applause,
The band plays to a rapturous encore.
Sadly the festivities are soon over,
The bride and groom depart for an island in the sun,
A paradise resort awaits them in Fiji,
Where they'll engaged in some honeymoon fun.

Fine Buliciri

I Hate Mornings All Over Again (And I'm Okay With That)

So I guess now that the hole isn't so jagged
And my voice doesn't break into a hush
On the second syllable of your name
Like I'm awestruck and not,
Heartbroken, (and shamed)
It must mean I'm ready to wake up one day
And forget about you

And now every day is a list of all the things
You didn't do and didn't say
A wake-up call every time I think abut
Everything I gave up and lost
Through ego (and doubt)
And I'm learning to hate the mornings again
Like I did before you came

But sometimes I have these thoughts of you
That I just can't box away for good
Because they belong to me and you and this
And you are mine, in a way
To remember (and miss)
And why should I forget the girl that I was.
When I thought I was yours.

And it was okay to walk with a spring in my step
Remembering the nights that came before
Like the heat of your hand on my thigh
And curling myself inward, into you
With a smile (and a sigh)
Because it wasn't worth it, with you
To be cold and brittle and hard

But I'm growing tired of the effort it takes
To remind myself constantly to forget and forget
And I'm ready to look back now and say
That I can't believe the bad poetry I wrote
About those early days
And I'll laugh and laugh so hard it will hurt
And it'll seem so easy then, how I learned to forget.

Lianne Lee

Destiny Of An Angel

The sounds of life continue to travel past,
As you daydream about a golden lass,
Eyes so pure, hair so soft and flowing,
Her presence a miracle in showing.

Her touch would stop a beating heart,
Her kiss would surely paralyse every part,
A wonderland of angels in one glimpse of perfection,
A shimmering dream in life's reflection,

A flower from the gods of tranquillity,
A ripple in the lake of complexity,
A new yearn, a new desire,
Wanting this angel to spark the fire,

She would whisper so soft to hypnotise,
A look so enchanting to immobilize,
Destiny could bring you together,
In this dream of the now and forever,

Walking the fields of harmony,
Would this angel be at one with me?
Or is the angel simply to send thoughts insane?
Or could destiny make our paths the same?

Until I know I lie and stare at visions through glass,
Daydreams of an angelic mystical lass,
Not hearing or seeing reality,
At least until awake I be.

Patrick Jefferies

Ode To Happiness

Would you like a slice of happiness?
Come, share our wedding cake
In doing so, be witness to the vows that we did make
To have and to hold from this day forward
In sickness and in health
For *us* this is all *we* need,
Love be our only wealth.

Elizabeth Fleischer

Fortress

Despite concrete walls and heavily bolted doors,
From fighting beasts with deadly jaws
And scary roars
All teeth and claws
And other wars,
With plans including fatal flaws
Breaking all the rules and laws
Through ice and storm and flooding thaws
From distant shores
With bleeding wounds and cuts and sores
Where heart pounds and sweat pours
To a lack of deafening applause
You walked right in and made me yours,
Just to make me yours.

Michele Amos

I Love You

My heart beats because you care,
My life is complete because you are there,
I want you forever, I love you so much,
I look forward to the moments I can feel your touch.

The world is full of people who are looking around
For that special something we have already found.
I'm lucky to have you, I'll keep you forever.
Loving you, caring for you, leaving you never.

Our future together is exciting and bright,
I dream of adventures through the day and the night.
To live all my life with you by my side
Is all that I want on life's roller-coaster ride.

To explore all the world, with your hand in mine.
To build a life with you, and spend all our time
Being happy together, whatever the weather.
All I want is you and to love you forever.

Kelly Louise Meacock

SEPARATION

We have to part and say goodbye
And although I smile I need to cry
One last kiss with lips I will miss
Sweet and tender my mind surrenders
But half broken-hearted I must say no This is the time I must kiss and go
Our time unfolds, this parting foretold
In secret we met, in silence I leave
In your tearful face I see you grieve
The past has gone, we must move on
Still in my heart are our sensual hours
Yet time has passed as withering flowers
In sad emotion there is a parting devotion
So as lovers we part with heavy hearts.

James Tracey-Burner

RED AS ROSES

Everything in me aches to touch him,
To feel the comfort solicited by a single touch.
Warm body – his hand would feel like sunshine on mine,
I reach out . . .
But one glance into his eyes,
And the familiar stars which twinkle there
Harden to splinters of stony ice,
And I can see it is not to be,
He can feel the eyes of others pressing in around,
Pushing, jostling,
We naturally strain 'gainst their ministrations.
Both of us. So it is not to be.

Rigid words snap out at me.
'Don't! Don't touch me.'
I curl up inside and cry tears which flush
Into my cheeks. Red.

Anna Hands

WHAT IS LOVE?

Was it not we, the poets,
That invented this cruel notion?
The false pretence of an emotion,
So wholly unattainable and yet,
In contradiction,
All consuming and smothering,
Completely destroyed,
Beautifully reborn.
The one thing that will rejuvenate,
And simultaneously be the end of us all.
What is love?
A word so easily pounced upon,
And offered up in hope,
To hook a companion,
To initiate sex,
To live, to lie, to give, to die.
We have made it too perfect,
No pour soul can ever meet,
The impossible criteria,
That governs what we,
Have made the world believe,
Are the requirements.
Though love is not necessarily about wants,
Needs or even desires,
It *is* necessary,
It is trust, faith and quite simply says:
I cherish you.

Kieran Davis

Inspired By The Oven Manual

Based on my feelings for you
While sad at the time – It's no longer the case
I'm happy and just don't feel blue

You made me feel beautiful – no one else did
You made me unburdened and pure
The loneliness caused by the playground of youth
Your happiness carried my cure

The gun of my pain ebbed a long time ago
So right here I will put it to bed
I am grateful to know you, you changed my heart
So now I will change my head

There is yet a chance I will love once again
And I hope this will one day be true
The danger is giving my love to another
Another who is not you

Dat Guy Dere

Lovelorn Optimist

I look in the mirror and now I see a broken disheartened me.
Once so fresh, bold and brass, my face shows of a heart collapsed,
the pain inside is new and firm, why don't we romantics learn.
Love is fleeting, love is blind, love isn't always so kind
but still we try to find that love,
that's talked about in all the books.
From Gone with the Wind to Wuthering Heights,
it's not that far away from our sights,
we still try to find that place where we can find the final embrace,
the one that lasts till the end of time or until the clock hits nine,
but where we find it isn't always clear and a surprise interaction could always be near.

Amy Hughes

Jailbird Love

I can listen to you lie
But every time another part of me will die
And another tear I will cry
Just like a gunshot to my heart
A bullet to my brain
But by your side I still remain

I'm told I deserve better
More than a jailbird and his monthly letter
Locked away for his violence
Without him around the house is filled with a deathly silence
No crashing plates
No drug-taking mates
Just me and my bruises

I know people think you're abusive
I know people think I'm stupid
Maybe even deluded
How can you help who you fall for?
But I can't withstand this love anymore

I am stronger than this
Not taken in by your kiss
I'll tell it to you straight
But I've left it too late

Now I am the reason you're in your cell
Accompanied to my farewell
Maybe it was just a possessive love
Now I can only be represented by a white dove

Stacey Hubbard

SPIKE

In clasped and shaking hands,
I held that spiked, vibrating thing
That so messily clacked from your tongue.
Snatched up and held at face level,
Surprised by the desire
To clench it close
And have it sting my palms.
And to know that right now
I couldn't drop it for the life of me.
Honestly –
It frightens me,
To watch my pen give body to this so willingly.
Yet I dress it up, tuck it away
Where your eyes are likely to miss –
I keep baulking,
But what I want to tell you is this;
I'm beyond doubt now.

Rebecca Taunton

SOMETHING SPECIAL

Something special for you and me
A special no one can see

Through difficulties, it may decide to break
A new one is made
Either give or take

To bring us closer
It's where we belong
And it may blow us away
But I will always remain strong.

Unbreen Shabnum Aziz

The Princess

There once was a princess
who lived in a high tower
surrounded by petrified trees
and spiky thorns
where majestic blue finches flew
and cavaliers graced the southern sky
they flew the heavens searching for damsels in distress

While deep at the bottom of the tower the serpent kings
circled the princess to keep her from harm
where Mellusina the water maiden danced
like a glittering bauble she shone brightly
waiting for her Prince Charming
One day after many years she was looking out
of her magic window

Her beautiful raven hair blowing in the evening breeze
Her black eyes glistened like shining stars
The people of the night began to sing
'A Starry Night'
An enchanted melody to capture her prince
A cavalier graciously flew by, stopped to listen
to the music and could not resist her ravishing beauty

His long black hair flew like luminous clouds
And he blew her a soft kiss of blustering dancing wind
that swirled magically
like a perfumed scent of falling rose petals

A gift for 'My True Love'
With one giant magnificent swoop
he picked her up
Like a knight in shining armour
and carried her into the night
to live happy ever after
in his castle in the sky.

Lorraine Hayley Mosley Coburn

Give But Can't Get Back

What are you fighting for?
You're still trying.
Already done crying. A long, long time ago.
But still the seeds you manifest grow.
You're getting old.
And you're still cold?
The building was sizzling,
danger everywhere.
Just like smoke
love hovered in the air.
They were clay before going out to play
and now they're grounded from being moulded.
Too big now to even hold it.
Life's a bitch and don't
you know it.

Aaron Noel

My Love

My love, you see the saddest colours only;
Your self-made image steeped in winter's grey.
This palette, almost monochrome, whilst pleasing
To my eye, does not recall your symphony
Of rainbows; this refracted light is glory
And the blending of your hues is happiness.
Until the myriad beams that dance and shimmer
Are aligned, no one can truly see your face.

My love, how strange that blue is melancholy
When the heaven of your eyes is painted thus;
I wonder if I am illusion's captive
Once deceived, now colour-blind and envious
Of those for whom no borders cause encumbrance
And for whom a single shade is revelry.
For I fear that, though these jewels are mine to worship,
In my heart I hide the guilt of ennui.

Jon Cooper

Love Hurts

Love hurts and breaks
the heart that aches
Love hurts and tears
the heart in shreds
Love hurts and makes
the heart lead and pound
Love hurts and makes
the heart rebound
Love hurts inside
one tries to hide
Love hurts and makes
one want to cry
Love hurts and sends
the head to the clouds
Love hurts like it
has no sound
Love hurts and
it can be so blind
Love hurts.

Peter Payne

Fifth Avenue

This shabby pit's alive tonight.
We wanderers flock to neon lights
And laugh for laughter long since dead,
And dance the words we never said.

We invented this;
This raucous bliss,
This weave of limbs,
This kiss.

And this is what it's all about;
Just the fact that we're all out.
I'm sure there have been deeper theories coined
Than 'arms round shoulders;
Voices joined'.

Adam Leese

The Price Of Reason

My mind is blank,
And yet is full of thoughts,
Where heart and brain do battle.

As ink is spread across this page,
A pain is spread inside;
I thought I made myself prepared,
That happiness will dwell within me!

Oh but how wrong I was to place my faith in Reason,
For now I feel that treacherous scum's treason!
Where are you now
When I most need you?
How come so quiet you've become?

He hides in silence somewhere in my mind,
Afraid to show his face,
For Reason's greatest fear,
Is our emotion's mace,
Which now but strikes me down . . .

Oh he will tell you many things,
When you're in state of harmony and peace,
But when you listen,
When you act;
He's nowhere to be seen.

You are alone;
You cannot think,
And yet, can't help but do so.

My heart's in flames,
It wants her back,
My mind is cool and cruel,
It says: 'What's done is done,
You've made your choice,
Now let the torture's drum,
Beat ever more within you.'

Nikolai Holding

VELCRO

Sometimes rejection is just as difficult to give as it is to receive.
Sometimes it clings to Velcro hands like a piece of wool.
And the wool gets caught up in the teeth of the Velcro,
so much so that it's impossible to stick two pieces of Velcro together because the wool is
tangled in-between.
Sometimes it's like that damp smell that is sometimes there
when the radiator doesn't work properly
so towels don't dry.
And it needs to be diffused but there's no air freshener.
Useless hands wave the smell in vain attempts to scatter it
but the ratio of air to smell is too unbalanced
so the smell remains.
Besides, Velcro hands don't wave very well
due to the lack of dexterity
so the smell gets caught up in the fibres of the wool
which just makes thing worse.
And it's like the smell and the wool will never go away.
It seems as though the severity of the situation would be so much less
had the hands not been made of Velcro.
Or if one of the hands was made of skin
and muscle
and bone
and veins
and arteries
and the other Velcro,
so the regular hand could at least use regular fingernails on regular fingers
to pick at the wool
and make a legitimate attempt to divorce wool from Velcro.
But what of the smell?
Perhaps if the nose was sliced off,
cut up,
and stored in a well-sealed Tupperware box,
the problem would be solved.
But surely the eyes and ears and mouth would then have to be severed and stored
accordingly,
in which case the hands would be useless anyway,
Velcro or no Velcro.
And the featureless face would curse the spite of the nose.

So maybe it has to be supposed
that if Velcro hands hold Velcro hands,
wool will get caught up in the teeth,
and the fibres of wool will become ragged and worn.
Perhaps some parts of the wool will fall from the Velcro's grasp,
or perhaps the wool will just slither out one day unexpectedly,
or get caught on another piece of Velcro.

Hannah O'Brien

At Your Most Restful

I awoke, and watched you sleep.
The way you simply
breathe.
And your eyes flicker beneath your lids as you dream,
I wonder if you dream of me.
You look at rest as morning dawns,
The dim grey sky outside is lightening,
Chasing away the last few distant stars.
To hold you like this forever,
In this moment contained in the strange
Early daylight.

I suddenly realise you're awake,
And are watching me watch you.
That wonderful small smile plays across your soft lips
And I return it,
As you pull me down to rest my head upon your chest,
Your hand strokes my hair, my shoulders,
Leaving spirals on my skin,
And together we doze, content,
With nowhere else we'd rather be.

Glynnis Morgan

Malnourished Heart

Left too long, without a beat
This malnourished heart is now deplete
You deprived it of love, even when we kissed
Trying on my own, I couldn't persist

You drained my rhythm, my passion for life
When all I wanted was to be your wife
To share our lives and create something new
To say you love me and really mean it, was all you had to do

And now my heart is dry and black inside
I surrender, in the knowledge that I tried
I may be missing a vital organ, and I may be somewhat weak
But a higher love, a better love, I will continue to seek

I pray that through time and experience, I will restore
As I continue strolling through this loving war

Ethan Chapples

Him

A curl in his hair, a crooked grin,
Round brown eyes, make shivers on my skin,
A mountain with no movement, but a heart of soft mist,
Listen to his music, it's like a single kiss,
He looks down to me, and I just gaze back,
Lost in your world, time lost track,
I will stay with you forever, I won't let go,
I know it won't be easy, we are star-crossed lovers don't you know?
Which path will we take? Left or right?
I won't leave, without a fair fight,
Hand in hand, fingers entwined
Where do we go? We have enough time
You're all I need, and your sweet tunes,
It's like you are my sun, and the moon.

Tabitha Lay

I Pray

To be kind and caring to you every day,
To listen to what you have to say.
I pray,
To always stay the same.
I pray,
Not to ignore you or rush past you,
I pray,
To always have time for you.
I pray we always have our candle of hope.

Aqeel Ali

Toenail Clippings

Your toenail clippings
Floating in the toilet
Your greying nose hairs
Dancing 'round the drain
The toaster you bought me for our anniversary, With the thousand knobs that drive me insane.

Your obsession with finding the cheapest deal
And not throwing out your holey socks
The way you roll and reel your toe jam
Just after I've swept the floors
The hours you spend doing a two-minute job,
And let's not forget that I asked you two years ago to fix the bloody key fob.

And then you wink at me.

You take my hand and we turn on Corrie
And I forget the toenails, toaster and nose hairs
It doesn't matter that we haven't spoken in thirty-two days
Because our intertwined fingers still make my heart sing
You look at me and no words are needed to be said
You have my heart, my soul, my body, even though you do in my head.

Swapna Haddow

Moribund

Anguish hangs in the silence.
Too late now for all those unsaid words,
To heal the wounds of time.
Oh, that I'd got here quicker.

Has the Reaper been already?
Is the harvest gathered?
Wait . . .
Almost imperceptibly,
The rise and fall of the bedcover betrays hidden life.
The faintest flicker.

Emerging from the shadows of the ward
A nurse.
'Try and sit up,'
A skinny wrist moves almost imperceptibly,
Flopping feebly back onto the bedcover,
As if the clear plastic tube snaking up to the saline bottle is too heavy.
Grey-blue lips emit a faint whispered response.
Or is it just a sigh?
It's impossible to tell.
Unfocused eyes register neither pain nor emotion.
The young nurse raises him slightly, gently,
Arms embrace bony hunched shoulders
Placing a spoonful of grey ooze between sealed lips.
It trickles uselessly down a stubbly chin.
She wipes it away.
And smiles.
'I'll leave it here for him . . .
He can have it when he's ready.'
I start to protest,
'He's very weak,' she interrupts.
'We can't force him . . .
He has to get his strength back first.'
She speaks to me as you would a child.
If only she knew!
I try once more to reason with her.
She smiles condescendingly again.
'We'll see . . . '
She moves away.
A shadow in the distance.
I get up to leave.

Next day he's curled up like a foetus.
Not even covered by the bed sheets.

It's been a week now.
I don't think he's tried,
Something died in him that night.
Even his beloved Mozart stirred no lingering emotion.
I regard the pathetic old broken husk
And see myself.
Without grief.
Without pity.

Harry Hunt

VACANT

Crowded places highlight isolation
Endless conversations soaked in commiseration
Desolate hearts looking for the solution
With no answer there is only confusion.

The child at school bullied and abused
Begging for company and always refused
A solitary jail cell immersed in darkness
Inside a guilty prisoner longing for forgiveness.

In the field the delicate rose resides
Endeavouring every day to collide
And waiting and believing oneself incomparable
A notion that a companion is attainable.

The sun sits awkwardly on the horizon
Only clouds show an ounce of passion
The moon soon replaces his acquaintance
Anticipating affection but losing patience.
Night morphs into day with a timeless touch
This one interaction lacks so much.

She rests on every inch of Earth
Surrounding people in irrational hurt
That immeasurable vacant feeling
Which battles against methods of healing,
Everyone is vulnerable and prone
To that inescapable reality: alone.

Stacey Reay

Isabelle

I met you on the island,
That's beautiful Corfu
And from the instant that I saw you
I knew our love would be true.

It may sound like a cliché
That it was love at first sight
But although you were a challenge,
Our first kiss came naturally that night.

We're now back in England
Still going good and strong
I hate how far away you live,
It really is so wrong.

When you leave me at the station
My mind becomes a mess,
I feel I have a problem
That only you can address

But when that week is over
I am myself again,
All my worries are forgotten,
All thoughts escape my brain.

Without you I am only
One half but not a whole
The next bit does not make sense but
It's my heart that you have stole.

I say you are my drug
To whom I cannot say no,
So I've come to the conclusion
I'd be a fool
To ever let you go.

Dan Long

My Heart Sings

I love you my dear with all of my heart
Without you here I'm just a spare part.
I think of you a lot throughout my day
I care for you more than I could say,
I count myself lucky to call you my own.
Even when we argue and you rant and moan.
I treasure each day I spend with you dearly
And I hope this message comes across to you clearly,
No matter if I try, to deny it's true
I don't want to be with anyone but you.

John Stewart

Red Rose

Yellow roses of friendship ripple in space,
The sun's beauty they each encase,
They fill the mind with joy and grace.

Some are yellow with a blush of red,
From tantalising thoughts and words left unsaid.
Should they go, or stay instead?

Some people say that life is too short,
And open their window to intoxicating thought.
So better be quick, than by time be caught.

The difference of red to yellow rose,
Is that of poetry to prose,
Nip the bud but the feeling grows.

Tonight although all is still,
The red rose flickers and wants its fill.
I'll let it grow. I'll let it thrill.

Some make love and some make lust.
Before my dreams all turn to dust,
For me, I'll show it's love I'll trust.

Nandita Keshavan

Dear Universe

You never did understand, my point of view,
Despite all the times, I tried to explain it to you.
Continuously spoken, again and again,
Friends would then question if I'd gone insane!
But I guess it just grew, a gradual progression,
The closer you got, the greater the obsession.
The more we interacted, my wall would grow thin,
Till eventually I gave up, I then let you in.
Expressed all my thoughts, drew out my mind,
Explained how you were the greatest, that I'd ever find.
Heartbroken and lonesome when you were not there,
Whilst in reality having not even experienced a stare,
But I knew it, I did, right from the start,
That you would soon acquire a significant place in my heart.
I tried to ignore it, completely let it go,
Like the atmosphere giving in so just pouring the snow.
I stood for a moment, should I stay or should I run?
But I was stuck in that orbit, like the Earth to the sun.
You held me close, I needed to breathe,
But that was the imagination my mind did perceive.
You really were far, a distance away,
When all I ever wanted, was for you just to stay.
Like a horse in a race, I'd conquered the hurdle,
Tried convincing myself that together we'd curdle.
Negativity took over, strongly captivating me
And then by surprise I'd untangled and ran free.
It felt so perfect, not under your spell,
But you were worlds away, you couldn't even tell!
To me I'd achieved, obtained that gold medal,
I'd driven away, shoved my feet on that pedal.
I learnt how it felt to just be unique,
So closed myself up to prevent a sneak peek.
All was successful, I'd defeated the sorrow,
Little did I know, what was lurking tomorrow.
Again you appeared, disguised as pure gold,
Arms outstretched, I was craving a hold!
I had a moment's thought, I was not going to play,
I'd save the future heartache, for a future day.
So I sighed, looked down and took a step back,
I was determined this time to stay on the right track.
Never again would I lie next to your chest;
Never would I conclude that you were the best.
No! I wouldn't drop another tear from my eye,

I'd just keep this space and hope you'd walk by.
I prayed for more courage, I believed I was strong;
But I fell once again, I had got it all wrong.
I eventually began to feel, what I had felt,
Like chocolate to heat you again made me melt.
Composure! I begged as I fell on one knee,
Don't toss and turn me like a ship to the sea!
I'd fallen again but there was nowhere to land,
Lost like one grain on a beach full of sand.
Cut from my family, they'd swatted the fly!
And this problematic dilemma was nobody's fault but I.
In solitude I wept and you'll often query why;
But I'll ignore the truth and instead utter a lie.

Nadia Bennett

Terrible Love

Never has love been portrayed
As constricting as this.
My shackles tighten,
With each tainted kiss.

Dependence is no virtue
When she won't let go.
This problem of love.
This craving below
For change. For freedom!
But my heart is tied
In a marriage of bondage,
To my faithful bride.

I've loved, and prospered,
But never at once.
My calls aren't answered
Except by silence.

Joseph Hankinson

AIN'T NO REASONING WITH LOVE

I ask myself time and time again,
I ask the Lord above.
Why I love you like I do,
but there ain't no reasoning with love.
I find loving you too difficult,
my mind can't reason with the pain.
They can't agree upon loving you,
when there's nothing at all to gain.
My love for you is an empty love,
it only goes one way.
It gives to you all it's got to give,
and my heart dies a little each day.
My mind screams, *it's useless girl,*
this you have to know.
But my heart pleads *it loves you,*
and will not let you go.
So each night I pray for its release,
to my Father up above.
Only to awake with you still there,
just ain't no reasoning with love.

Mary Webb

KEEP ME IN REMEMBRANCE

Keep me in remembrance
That's all I ask of you
Think of me as one, who was
Devoted fond and true
Do not let the passing years blot
Out the memory, or dim recollections
I prized so tenderly

Keep me in remembrance, so that
When I come again
I will find you as you were, my
Own may you remain
Let the old love still continue
Though we are far apart
Do not fail forget me not
And keep me in your heart.

Douglas Drummond

LOVE

What kind of love is this?
Emotions, stirring of the heart.
Depth of feelings deep within
Yes, love, unfathomable,
Stirring of the heart.

Love, a quantity of emotions,
Brought about from within.
Expressed in numerous ways,
The chemical changes of the heart,
The whole body doth affect.

Love, a *mystery* generated,
Often unaware.
Sights, smells, expressions.
Body language, stimulates
Stirrings of the heart.

Emotions, awakened, unleashed.
The ingredients of love amplified.
Outward evidence of the within,
Seen, felt, aware of love.
The emotions of the heart.

Rev Ralph A Watkins

KEEPSAKE

We do not remember days
We remember moments.
How beautiful a day can be
When kindness touches it.
Because of you, everything is so much nicer.
You have been my spouse,
My lover, my best friend, my confidante.
Being loved deeply by you gives me strength.
Loving you deeply gives me courage.
You have stolen my heart forever.
My romantic dreams pale
With the reality of you.
My soulmate and best friend.
You complete me.

Beverly Maiden

I Want To Marry Daisy

I want to marry Daisy
But my parents disagree
I think she's wonderful
And I'm sure that she loves me
She has that loving smile
I'm sure you would agree
My parents smile indulgently
Which damn well annoys me
It's getting out of hand
Cos they just don't understand
I do want to marry Daisy
I know I'm doing right
They annoy me so
I'm putting up a fight
They say just wait a while
We'll talk later about when
I don't want to wait
I'm already nearly ten.

Martin Selwood

Eternally Yours

From somewhere I have found the strength to finally admit to myself
That I shall always love you regardless of anything else
They say to love is to let go,
But that is only physically and not emotionally so.
I still desire you like the first time and that will always be true
Because that's nothing that time and space can ever erase
The way I feel about you

You never returned my passion or love
But then . . . you never said that you would
'I won't make promises I can't keep' you said,
But how I wished that you could
I tried to forget you and that was wrong,
Because it's something I just can't do
And though my life does go on
Forever . . . my only love, will always be you.

Paula Holdstock

VALENTINE

The Lord is strength and one's shield too
Be young, be foolish, be happy, be you
A country of candy and flowers to view
On Valentine's Day true friendship does brew
The Earth is full of unfailing love
Love and faithfulness the solution there of
Peace have they who love for sure
May those who love be so secure
One does love those who does love one
Patience and kindness is brought upon
Love does cover all the wrongs
And lengthen too as one prolongs
Love never fails so love each other
True love does spread to one another
'You truly love me more than these?'
Words now becoming regular pleas
For so many souls receiving there are
Waiting for true love and what they prefer
Serve one another in love sure do
Love never fails, it sees one through
So great is love for those who fear
Serve one another in love severe
Love covers all that is done wrong
Supporting one with strength to go on
Knowledge puffs up but love builds up
With the Valentine's Day champagne cup.

James Thompson

LOVE

Love is worth saving, I think you should know
But if we never fall in love then how can we grow?
How can an hour feel like a day
When the person you love is so far away?
When you hope that that person feels the same too
That that person is sitting there thinking the same about you
That it'll be alright, you'll see in the end
That love is worth sharing and to us it will send
A message of hope that will see our way through
But after all's said and done, we know what to do
We take it and hold it and make it grow strong
And keep it together so it never goes wrong
We think of the days when we laugh and hold hands
And think of the love that is cleansing our lands
Think of the times when you're bursting with joy
You feel like a child with their first Christmas toy
You think of the time that's coming our way
And hoping that love is coming to stay
But we've been there 'n' done that and let's not pretend
That love is our saviour, our guidance, our friend
Love can be rotten and hurtful and cruel
So when it raises its head, you know it's a duel
But you have to sit back and let it fit like a glove
Open the door and welcome in
Love
Please

Paul M Clarkson

THE WEDDING DAY

The morning arrived for our special day,
There were lots of things to do no time for delay.
The hairdresser was coming around half past ten,
To do everyone's hair, except for the men.
The bride was excited and frightened as well.
So many stories of this day people did tell.
The flowers arrived laid out in a case,
They had to be fresh, they must be in a cool place.
Outside the weather was bright but it was cold.
Guests started to arrive at the time they were told.
The house it was full not a spare yard to be had,
When will those cars arrive oh I will be glad.
Then off to the church all the guests go.
The house becomes quiet for a moment or so.
As into a chair we gratefully sink.
This gives us time and we start to think.
The bride is upstairs getting ready with Mum.
Downstairs the father grabs another small glass of rum.
Then the bride is ready he hears her coming down,
All dressed up in her flowing wedding gown.
Then they are alone just father and daughter.
Her eyes all sparkling as the sunlight it caught her.
He felt so proud his eyes filled with tears.
What or where had gone all those loving young years.

Barry Scott Crisp

NICOLE

Burning embers of virgin love heighten and ascend,
Transition into adulthood, one summery weekend.
A time long gone, but always near, always close at heart,
My birth to manhood, holiday fling, doomed from the very start.

Family holiday by the sea, Scottish seaside town,
In the penny arcade I was, just putting the pennies down.
In she walked, angel in red, little brother by her side,
Couldn't take my eyes off her, even though I tried.

She caught my gaze, embarrassed flush, smile comes back my way,
Eternity spent, just standing there, thinking of what to say.
Courage comes, I walk on up, I smile and ask her name,
Give her brother pennies galore, to go and play a game.

She takes her brother back now, to her parents on the beach,
We walk and talk, laugh and play, her hand I make a reach.
Now hand in hand, we stroll along, strange feelings take control;
I float on air, with gormless grin, as I walk with my Nicole.

After disco dancing frenzy, and moonlit kiss on sand,
I walk her back to caravan, head on shoulder, hand in hand.
We plan to meet the next day, by the children's penny arcade,
Another kiss, a fumbled feel, nothing more is said.

The next day's even better, the best day of my life,
Till what she suddenly tells me, cuts through me like a knife.
She's leaving me this day, her family's going back,
And the realization hits me, with an almighty blinding whack.

She senses my deep sorrow, takes me to the dunes below,
Where we consummate our teenage love, before she has to go.
I watch now as she's leaving, passing in the car,
My heart ripped out, teary eyed, with first emotional scar.

Those days will never leave me, never fade away,
My Nicole is always with me, always here to stay.

James Howden

ASPECTS OF Love - A Collection Of Poetry

A Gift Of Love

Love is about trusting one another,
Supporting each other, my best mate, wife and a wonderful mother.
The smile as you greet me is of a natural light,
And a kiss as we say goodbye or goodnight.

The team bond we have to help our sons each day,
Doing everything in the most simple way.
The four of us love our days out,
Spending time on a beach or just driving about.

After a bad day, when everything has gone wrong,
You will listen and I can talk, on and on . . .
Cuddles at the right time is a special gift,
And this helps each other like a huge lift.

Showing our appreciation is the smallest job to do,
I would be lost and incomplete without you.
Eight years of marriage has just flown by,
Knowing I am one happy and content young guy.

Love is not simply given to anyone,
You have to work at it and have plenty of fun.
We get stronger day by day, week by week,
Still extremely young and at our peak.

Adrian Bullard

Love Me

Take my hand
and hold my heart
keep I close to you
wrap me up
and keep me safe
release me from my gilded cage
and protect me
like no other
forever . . .

Paula Greene

LOVE

Love flows as ice when rain melts snow
It flows evenly to the smallest place
From head to heart 'n' every digit 'n' toe
Love is true in trust 'n' grace
It makes each home a happy place
Love for each other fills your special space
Both make a pledge for lasting life
To love, honour and obey
First the husband then the wife
The knot is tied till you're old 'n' grey

Love is as water in ice and ice as in water
Freezing to melt again shapeless without form
Love is beauty 'n' grace as each child is born
It is not solid but can be felt
One's love flows forever true
True love shall never melt.

Tom O'Mara

LOVE IS THE PRISM OF LIFE

Ten seasons now since love's bright prism died,
Life's colour ebbed. A cloudy drabness fell,
And shadows crept across my empty soul
With darkened fingers, casting hues aside.

How strange it seems that all still moves, while here,
Beside an inner lake of unshed tears,
Fond memories reflect of bygone years,
Not seen by other eyes; to me so dear.

The beauty of the world remains, beset
With all the joys of children's love,
Kind thoughts and words, fine gifts and deeds to prove
The precious kindliness of friends; and yet

When love that forms life's prism slips away,
Alas, one dwells in monochromes of grey.

Rev Prof John Beazley

MORTAL LIFE, IMMORTAL LOVE

If I should die let it be in your arms,
And be comforted by your loving charms,

If I should die let it be by your side,
So we can exchange our love from inside,

If I should die let me kiss your sweet lips,
And feel the passion before my life slips.

If I should die let me feel your warm touch,
The final embrace that will mean oh so much.

If I should die let it be with your love,
To take with me, on my journey above.

If I should die let the last thing I see,
Be your unique and everlasting beauty.

When I have died I want you to know
That I shall meet you when it's your time to go.

Anthony David Beardsley

LOVE SUCKS

Cupid is not such an innocent fellow,
That to me, at last, is plain.
Love can get awfully complicated,
I've only recently learned;
When Bob loves Sue and Sue loves Bill
And Bill loves Jane,
Nothing is resolved, all are frustrated,
And everyone gets burned.

An unresolveable, unending carousel,
Spinning until all are tired;
And what makes me feel stupid
And probably the maddest,
Of all the useful knowledge that
I've recently acquired,
Is that cute, chubby, cuddly, little Cupid
Is a bleeding psychopathic sadist!

John Bliven Morin

RELEASE ME

You cannot feel,
yet hold more compassion
than any living soul.
You don't wish for my pain,
yet never interfere.
Without you, I am lost.
Sadly, I can not feel your touch,
as deeply as I need to.
Your love is unconditional,
yet I've never felt more alone.
Hold me close in your arms.
I beg of you, release me from my bondage,
of each day's silent misery.
It is impossible for you.
You are here with me constantly,
and you see how I suffer.
The pain has become unbearable.
I wish to not breathe air.
Internal conflict that no one can stop,
not even you, unless
it is not my time to go.
Then and only then,
you're capable to interfere.
For you are not mortal,
but a celestial angel.
Please, take me to Summerland,
Paradise or Heaven,
where pain does not occur.
Because, as I walk through the shadow
of the valley of death,
I beg for you to release me,
of all the heartache I have endured.

Dori Wheeler

Earth-Sky

Summer has burst into song,
on your skin is the scent of the universe,
and for a while – not long –
we shall forget winter, white and terse.

Down on beds of grass we lie,
and as our bodies kiss warm soil
Earth becomes the endless sky,
while limb by limb our roots uncoil.

Will Martin

That's Almost Enough

Friends of single lonely people
Can see cats purring in annoying lies
With flavour touching mosaician eyes
Inside the communications that twist
From elasticised plethoras
While they're nothing but very boring

For the entrusted super eccentrics
Quarantined inside the machine
Opening criticise those incumbents
For saying they might do!
Whereas outside they never ever see
The escalating retractions any deeper

Ambling through and touch the forest
As life around the mystic indemnities
Might come back to remind some
That pretty looks melt into love
And recurring dreams from confusing hopes
Identify how we want to read the meanings

Am I blessed every time I sleep?
Or am I just marking my time
Till the day comes when I'm fluent
And the proud pedestal I once built
Becomes reachable after all
With the excruciating despair at last defeated

Thomas McDougall

As He Loves

I thought that love when it came,
would be perfect in every degree,
two hearts that sought the same,
but that was not what happened to me.

From the first the tensions grew,
we both brought baggage from our past,
we tried so hard to see it through,
but alas we parted at last.

We tried to remain good friends anon,
but eventually we drifted apart,
it seemed that precious love was gone,
but God had other plans for my heart.

I came to see where we had gone wrong,
the reason love had gone downhill,
love isn't of the heart as in a song,
true love is actually an act of your will.

You must love as the Father loves,
unconditionally, unselfish and free,
feelings as gentle as snow-white doves,
there is no 'I' in 'We'.

Love does not hate, or argue or mistrust,
it sees only good and purity,
not giving in to greed and lust,
a love like His can set you free.

And now our hearts are again entwined,
with no barriers to make one stumble,
Love like Him and you will be fine,
Love empowers only when you're humble.

Bill Hayles

Love Doesn't Die

Love doesn't die!
It just gets pushed down,
Somewhere dark and deep,
Somewhere hurt and sore.
The damage done for those still yet to come,
By the one that came before.
Yet every now and then
Something sparks a memory,
And in that moment,
That memory of loving eyes
Tender lips, a warm embrace,
I know I still love her.
And even still,
After all this pain,
Could even love her more
Love doesn't die!
It just gets pushed down deep,
Somewhere dark,
Hurt and sore
The damage done for those still yet to come
By the one that came before.

Robin Martin-Oliver

The Faery Ball

The Faery Ball of summer's night,
Calls the rose to bloom,
Sets their golden blood alight,
With the chime of a midnight moon.

The Faery dance leaves roads in the sky,
A maze of pink shimmering dust,
It pours silent and stillicide,
Until the break of morning's hurricane rush.

But, sometimes, the anti-clockwise wind
Draws back the rose to bud,
And the silver-tipped Faery wing
Freezes with the golden blood.

Rachel Hughes

THE CASTAWAY

Dialling the familiar number
Hearing the ringing tones
That no one picks up
Sending letters full of love
To 'that' address known by heart
Only to have them returned unopened.

Standing outside the house
Broken windows of the soul
Declare there's no one in
Introspective in 'her' room
No perfume now or familiar odour
Nor dressing table clutter.

Leaves underfoot crunching, wrinkled, spent
The mottled tones faded as old skin
The hushed thought, and
Sudden realisation, that
She-is-gone, transparent
Through that other door . . .

Adrian G McRobb

FLUTTER ON BY

Flutter by butterfly for love resides no more,
The desert plains sing again, for it's a-calling on the moors,
So float a' by oh butterfly and rest those delicate wings,
As I'll no longer kiss your heart, where the heavens weep and sing,
Oh, fly on high to the tranquil blue, for I am bruised and bled,
As in the morn in isolation, I shall awaken from these depths,
So by this window solemnly I can only sit in wait,
For another butterfly to flutter by, and contentment impregnates.

Carly Burns

A Sensual Moment

Warm touch leads to sensation
Of dreamy, drifting elation
As hormones react to mingling
Responding to the tingling
Glanced, by half-open eyes
In the place where passion lies
Gentle shivers
As tender body quivers
And fingertips deliver
From the touches of the lover's giver
How the moments drift
From that sensual gift
To a heated writhe
Where immaculate feelings thrive
Uncontrollable pleasure
The moment of the measure
Deep, with moved mortal soul
With no control
And how the body aches
Moment shakes, as flesh quakes
To sweet rapture
Of the instant that those seconds capture
Relaxation
Of fired, but satisfied perspiration
A happy lay to sleep
Of the physical sensation, so deep
Taste of love, now satisfied
No tenderness denied.

Terry John Powell

Festival's End

5.50am 26 August
Edinburgh

Sleep on a little longer yet,
Let not the day confront my eyes too soon.
Still let me gaze a little while
On stolen shared serenity
That once was our possession as of right.
And let me warm myself once more
On dying embers of the flames
That once burned incandescent in your soul.
Permit me one more time to stand and gaze
On blood-red cirrus clouds
And gliding gulls on mourning winds
Until the morning steals the silhouettes
Of castle walls and towering cliffs
And splashes careless colours on the day.

Sleep on a little longer yet
Allow me to believe a moment more
In fairy tales and magic spells
And dragons slain by power of truth
And love that lasts eternally;
At least until the city wakes
And traffic noise burns off the night,
Till morning shines on towering cranes
That flaunt their rule on building sites,
And in aggressive self-importance
Break the flowing metre of the skyline.

Sleep on a little longer yet.
Let not the day affront serenity too soon.
Still let me stand a moment and pretend
From vantage point of elevated peace
The city dances highland jigs
Postponing summer's end another day.
Let joyful songs still resonate
While juggling buskers toss my thoughts
And catch my soul with elegance
Then stop a while to bow for my applause.

Sleep on a little longer yet
And, resolute for now, I shall pretend
And fool myself another lifetime more
That morning does not summon you,
The festival has time to run
And we are not in Edinburgh on borrowed time.

Michael Forester

Heaven On Earth

A B C
It's just you and me,
And that's all that we need,
If you always follow I'll always lead,
The spaces between my fingers are meant to be filled by you,
You've got me mesmerized by all the things you do,
My heart's got your name all over it,
Two souls combining in perfect harmony because we're a perfect fit,
All across the world from coast to coast,
Baby it's always you that I'll love the most,
From the summit of the tallest mountain to the bottom of the sea,
Against all odds together forever you and me,
This is Heaven on Earth and I'm floating on a cloud,
I just can't contain my happiness, I want to shout it loud,
Your love's what gives me the strength I need to get by,
And without it my life would be meaningless and my heart would die,
There's not a thing in this world that could change my mind,
True love is like a small piece of Heaven on Earth, it doesn't come around often and it's rare to find,
I want to spend the rest of my life with you by my side
Laughing through the good times and drying the tears that I cried,
Nothing can ever replace the feeling because what can compare to Heaven and Earth combined into one,
I hereby promise to still happily be standing next to you when everyone else has gone.

Jennifer Louise Hudson

Never Forgotten: - $ilvee

I tried writing poetry as beautiful as you
But I've come to understand that this is something I cannot do
Cos the words to describe how I feel don't exist
So as a compromise I have made a list.

Although I know you're perfect
I love you not for this,
But instead for any imperfections
That make you who you are.

You see now I know you're modest
And won't agree if I call you a 'goddess',
But to that I say that no one is without fault
Definitely not myself, nor you and not anybody else.

I love that you don't tell lies.
I love the way you squint your eyes
Leering at me in a judgmental way
For something I do or something I say.

However I loathe it when you call me 'dude',
I don't know why . . . I just find it rude.
Though to be honest I have no objection
To you labeling me a 'tard'
Cos I know it is meant lightheartedly as an act of affection
And has no intention to leave me scarred.

I love the sounds that you make when you eat
And I love to pass comment on your peculiar feet.
I love the numerous inside jokes that we share
Like the 'crow' 'crapstone' and even your 'hair',
Also your reluctance to say the word 'yeah',
And our many attempts to make ourselves scared.

I love that you are always so rosy
And am in fact intrigued myself
To know why it is you're so nosy,
Although I suppose people say 'knowledge is wealth'
Which means you can pay for me for once
Because intelligence is something you have an abundance of.

Whenever we'd go surfing your maternal instinct took over
As you embraced anxiety that I would come down with hypothermia.
Just because my lips turned blue
And my speech slurred.
But truth be told one hug from you
And I am cured.

ASPECTS OF *Love* - A Collection Of Poetry

I hate to see you cry, even when they're tears of bliss
Cos instantly I'm left helpless
As I can only offer a shoulder to catch your tears,
And an oversized ear to take your fears.
At which time my lips will not speak a word
Of the private matters that I have heard.

I love the way your hair feels against my face
But can't say the same about its taste.
Plus I suppose it's no surprise that it smells heavenly
After all you are an angel sent to me like it is destiny.
Cos there must be a reason we met socially
And it can't al be down to Amberley
Because let's face it, she aspires to be a footballer's WAG
And it isn't hard to say that she can be a shiag.
Also I don't like that you don't seem to trust me
Cos I feel that I have proven that I am trustworthy
Though I guess a few mistakes from the past
Will come back to bite me in the ass
So I now attempt to make amends for my four
Wrongs, and prove myself to you once more.

I'll be with you through the good times,
With you through the bad,
With you when you're happy
And with you through the sad.
Even when we're miles apart
I will always be close to your heart . . .
In your breast pocket; on your phone
So you needn't ever feel alone.

I must apologise if there's anything I've left out
And I hope this poem crushes any doubt
You have about me and the true feelings I have.
But if you need any reassurance that I've only three words to add.

Darren James Lee

THE LADY OF MY DREAMS

The words spring from thy cherry lips,
A flow of gentle breeze.
The soft gaze that thou give,
The look of 'if you please'.

The shapes of thy very breasts,
Two orbs that nurture life:
Such bosom of smooth complex
Bringeth admiration to one's sigh.

The protrusion of thy very thighs,
Glide elegantly under thy robes.
Thy virginity, so pure and bright,
Doth many attempt to probe.

Changjiang Zhang

TO MY VALENTINE

I'm seeing your face for the very first time; I'm holding your gaze with my heart
I need to explain just how much I love you, how much it has grown since the start
How lucky am I that you still care for me, if you did not I surely could tell
Beside you's enough, and when times were tough, you rescued me each time I fell
I do like your style, I do like your smile, your chuckle just makes me feel warm
Your eyes sparkle bright, when I bid you goodnight, I can't wait to see you each dawn
So thank you my love for being my friend, my companion for all these great years
With you by my side for the rest of my days only joy will still bring me to tears
Love you.

Graham Hayden

Love's Dream
(For my wife, Janet)

Love's dream is to love
Dreams of the way for love
Gives all that love sees
There never is love but love

We wait all the moment for love
Hours, days, months, years
Love will arrive for you
Will love receive or go?

Love can and will go
Hold on for the moment of time
Love races through the mind
Your heartbeat's in tune

Pain or ecstasy increases
Love can give happiness
Love takes and kills love
What love gives and leaves

A scream in the darkest night
Love can give peace
To any broken heart or spirit
We strive for love's peace

You give your arms and soul
For love that is given and needed
Love's dream is to love
And to give love to love

Is all the dreams of love

Ian Cresswell

The Path

I wander down the path
My life the uncharted way before me
Each step I take anew
Is upon virgin territory

Yet I walk alone

It is a new dawn I awake to each day
Bringing a hope yet to be fulfilled
What I search for I do not now
But always onward I seek and yearn

Yet still I walk alone

Others sometimes walk with me
Sharing their hopes and their fears
Opening my eyes and my mind
To things I would never have seen
Showing me just what I could truly be
Supporting me through the years.

Yet even then I walk alone

The land changes under my feet
Time passes and seasons change
Life begins for some
Their first steps unsure and unsteady
They walk before me on my path, making it their own
But for others it brings a welcome end
A rest from a long journey

Yet once more I walk alone
I have walked this world all my life
I have lived and loved and dreamed
I've learned to see through other's eyes
And shared all that I have seen

Yet I deserve to walk alone

So now at last at the journey's end
I look back and I realise
No matter what I have done
That I have always known
You were always with me

And I never walked alone.

Peter Madden

ENDEARING LOVE

Now we are older
Have mellowed with time
Look back to our young years
When we feel inclined
The wee early mornings
The school run each day
The holidays, beaches
We traveled away
The many adventures
The people we met
Of memories gathered
And love and respect
Enthusiasm, energy
Put into each day
The sweet lovely times
Now so far away
Our children have grown up
And made their own way
Now grandchildren
Giving us pleasure each day
Where we are at
Is a good place to be
The closeness and love we share
Tender and sweet
The memories treasured
The sweet happy days
With endearing love
To last all our days.

Jeanette Gaffney

VALENTINE

Love that clings like barbed wire,
Blood that burns, etched in fire
The sentimentality of brambles and thorns,
Promises twisted echoes and scorns,
More an icy grip
Of fingers that rip,
And strip at sinew and bone.

Elaine Catherine Christie

YOU ROCK MY BOAT

You have given me hope. How can that be?
I can't quite believe this happening to me.
A kindred spirit, so far away,
Yet you feel closer every day.

Embarking on a new journey of friendship and laughter.
It maybe, we are a stepping stone to the 'ever after'.
Your words bring happiness to me
And I believe our friendship is meant to be.

May it overcome the distance that keeps us apart.
For you have a very special place in my heart.

Donna Giblin

TODAY IS THE DAY

Today is the day
And that is why my blood is fizzing in my veins
And the chambers of my heart tango, causing me exquisite pains
And all my cares like pigeons flap away.

Today is the day,
Which explains the taste of tin, nerves as taut as wire,
This huge joy and helpless grin, belly full of hunger and desire
To know you and love you in every way.

Today is the day,
Even the sun in all its colours and the birds
In song, the sound of water falling and the joy of words
And music cannot make me feel this way.

Today is the day
Which I do now have: whether love is long or short
And whether it is right or wrong or mostly lives in flesh or thought
Or spirit, it is where I want to stay.

Today is the day.

William Forsyth

To Those Of You Who Laugh And Ask Questions

He has an incredible voice
I could sit
And I could listen
To those tones flowing up
And down
All night.
And I have.

I have laid in his arms
Hidden safe from
The watching eyes
Of the stars
Safe in his arms
And listening to
His breath
Flowing up
And down.

So,
To those of you who laugh
And ask all those questions
I really don't care what you think
All the while we lay
In perfect harmony
With tones and breath
Flowing, and hidden from the stars
I will not need you at all
Nor care what you think.

Sam Sebbage

The Return Of Camelot

Watch out, here I come, an intergalactic, telepathic,
Cosmic being of light. Riding in on the cosmic
Highway to enchant your soul and sowing the seed
Of cosmic love into your heart and letting it flow away
Forever out into the cosmos of eternal oneness.

Bringing you the power and magic that is your spirit,
Open up to a world of enchantment and wonder as it
All unfolds so beautifully around you. Feel the magic
Flow through your entire being as you are swept away
In my love that is forever eternal.

I come for you now in this moment in time. It is our
Destiny to be united again as one because you turned
Over the last page and saw the future of our dreams
Come into reality. Listen to the poetic heartbeat in my
Pen as it leaves a cosmic trail of love in your heart and soul.

I bring to you the new age of Camelot in all its magnificence,
There is magic in the air, you can feel it enveloping your senses
And wrapping you up in its mystical embrace. It is the dream of your heart, with every breath you breathe in and every step you take
It is all revealed you to you in all its beauty and glory. The magic is back.

Starchild Moondust

WHERE ARE YOU?

Where are you?
What, at this moment, do you do?
Do you think of me?
Do you think of me as I do of you?
Are your dreams also filled with the same things you wish were true?
How does the sky above appear to you?
Does it speak to you of love, or make you cry?
Perhaps it seeks to make you sigh?
It takes me away, that much I can say,
To places where I can wonder, as I often do of your face:
Moments that can tear me asunder.
And the fear, through the years, has not been quite absent;
But always present, even if at times out of mind, is regret,
My closest friend who lets me never forget;
Who, true-blue, will make all this a tale without end,
Subsisting gratuitously – or maybe graciously?
Is it I who insists on this? Do I wish it to continue?
Because it has been you?
Will always be you?
I would much like that I knew for certain,
That the haze raised, this heavy curtain before me.

Mark Mikkelsen

Love Poem

I'm trying to write a love poem
From memory, not the present date
I'm toying with all the clichés
Indiscretions have sealed my fate

How could I throw our love away
When life marched to our beat?
My lines smack of ruination
Regrets scattered over my feet

Tomorrow is a series of yesterdays
Don't seem able to inch ahead
My pen stays idle in my grasp
While I torment about what was said

I calculate the lifeless phone
Will picking it up answer any thing?
And as I stare at the empty page
What good will fine words ever bring?

I'm trying to write a love poem
Knowing there's no point at all
Every argument plays in my head
Every time I'm the one who falls

Why try to write a love poem?
What's the point of this exercise?
It all comes down to hindsight
When the foolish sound so wise.

Bernard Harry Reay

The Love Of My Life

As you wrap your arms around me so tight,
when everybody is watching that's in sight.
For you to kiss me on the cheek,
as it's only your love that I seek.
When I'm with you I feel whole,
and you get rid of all my black, sorrow and coal.
You are the most beautiful man I have seen,
and I know many men, that I have seen.
You fill the hole in my heart,
I love you so, and finding it hard to start.
I see mysteries in your eyes,
but in my heart you will never die.
If you ever go, I don't know what I would do,
you will leave me hurt, shocked and feeling so blue.
I will love you until the day I die,
I hope this is forever and not goodbye.
I think you're so very sweet,
and the best guy to ever meet.
Hopefully I will see you soon,
so I can kiss you under the moon.

Neil Douglas Tucker

Broken Heart Restored

Laughing, loving, living,
You were always giving,
Only once did you take,
You took my heart and made it break.

For weeks after I did weep,
The future seemed so very bleak
Until a better love came along
One that can be found in many a song.

I've been in love with it before,
And now my faith it does restore.
No matter where I may be,
It'll always be right with me.

It makes me laugh, it makes me cry
Never leaves me asking why.
Forever faithful it shall be,
Always together, music and me.

Charlotte Murray

Mask Of Emotions

The memories which I keep,
Thinking of you,
When I can't find sleep,
Lying here,
Wishing you were by my side,
Masking emotions,
But from my true feelings thee is no place to hide.
Dreaming of what can never be,
As time goes,
It's all too clear to me,
Yet those few moments we shared together,
Close to the heart forever,
And for those brief hours in time,
I was yours,
And you were mine . . .

Gavin Cooke

Careless Rockets

We are flying above the world tonight
Our troubles rush past us like the wild winds in our sights
I can't think of anyone else I'd share this moment with
Like careless rockets, we race through the sky so bright

I don't want to stay here anymore
I want to take off in my quest to explore,
All the new adventures that are there to see
So, will you come along with me?

I need to find the courage within the stars above
I need to see what it takes to fall in love
And when the time comes to show my pride
I will always ask for you to stay by my side

They won't show me what's right and what's wrong
But I am going to show them that I'm strong
Because you are the one who made that way
And I'm hoping that's how it's going to stay

Tonight is the night we leave arm in arm
Together we will embrace the cloud's charm
With no destination, we may travel quite far
For careless rockets is what we are.

Stephanie Caldwell

Nanny's Love

It's only been a short while since you and I first met
But oh! That feeling took me by surprise,
For there in my arms you lay, just a babe
I couldn't stop the tears as I looked into your eyes.
I whispered softly words tender and sweet
As I held you close, and rocked you gently,
All the memories of birth, flooded my mind
My love for you growing in my heart with every beat.

What fate awaits us, we will never know
Yet, of one thing I am certain,
As you grow and learn before my eyes
No matter what will come, my darling grandson
I will forever love you so.

Sue Meredith

A Cry In The Dark

As I lie in my bed in the dark
Your face dances wildly before my eyes,
Flashes of your smile thrill for a while
Can you not hear my cries?

When you left it was a hard thing to do
Remembering all those happy years
That we had faced as we lovingly embraced
Forgetting hardship and tears.

I loved you with passion divine
Burning with a fond desire,
Fanned by a romantic wind
Setting my whole body afire.

My mind thinks only of you
How wonderful it all used to be,
While you romance with somebody new
Think occasionally of me.

As I lie here alone in the dark
The image of you floats before my eyes,
Please come back, is all I can say
Can you not hear my cries?

Roy Hare

The Soul

Love is a feeling, a wretch to the soul
The pain, the joy, it's a wretch to the soul
I met him on a Monday, my heart stood still
Was he the one or was it a thrill
No words were spoken, had I realized my goal
Or was it another, wretch to the soul
Valentine's Day, came and went
He was the one, Heaven had sent
I met him that Monday he looked bleak
He didn't speak, I knew he was weak
He'd met someone else a 'Valentine's Love'
He couldn't help it, he'd fallen in love
Is this the end, had I played out my role,
Valentine's Day, another wretch to the soul.

Elizabeth Corr

DOWN TO EARTH

I said, 'You see that star on the far horizon?
Well that's Venus.'
'You're wrong,' she replied, 'That's just a pretty star
But don't let it come between us.'
Then a while later, someone told me it was Jupiter
And if you look carefully on a clear night,
You'll see surrounding it, three pinpricks of light –
Which are its moons.
So I told her this and she said,
'I don't give a damn about your silly planets!'
So having failed to impress with matters planetary and stellar,
I try once more and tell her
Something which makes her want to frown,
That as the sun goes down,
The orange glow is just atmospheric pollution.
Again she couldn't give a damn –
So this was my solution . . .
No cold nocturnal vigil in the observatory,
But on our trajectory in the candlelit conservatory,
I'm in cahoots with a burning star that shoots,
As we add to the sky's stardust,
With a big bang of exploding lust,
Seeing sizzling stars before our eyes,
Whilst we devour our pie in the sky.
Then for afters, I didn't want to warn her,
Before diving into her 'Muller Fruit Corner',
That if she ever left, my heart would be lost on a distant planet,
Not that she had planned it,
And I'd run rings around Saturn
If ever this should happen.
So instead, I'll build a tower as tall as I am able,
Higher than the one at Babel,
So she can touch the stars on a frosty night
And see close at hand for her delights,
Those meteorites, satellites and strange flashing lights.

Huw Parsons

His Love Overflows

Will she go or will she stay?
I seem to ask myself almost every day
She won't answer only stare
Will I get an answer to my prayer
Love is how I feel inside
She won't listen only hide

Love is how it has to be
Why won't she answer me
I live for each day that we might share
If only she could show she could care
I ask myself how long this can go on
Should I stay or should I be gone

Love isn't easy it's like a drug
Once you've fallen you're completely hooked
If I see you tomorrow will I know what to do
I could feel very happy or might may make me blue
She'll just ignore me and keep out of view
I just keep wondering what can I do

I'll pack my bags and leave her a note
Will she come and search for me this is what I hope
My life should be very happy I could be very glad
If only she would tell me then I wouldn't be mad
If only she would tell me what I want to hear
Instead all I get is silence which doesn't make it very clear

I've played every kind of love song
From ballads, blues and rock
Put some tracks together just to help me get along
Will I get an answer please
Only love will keep you strong.

Angela Wells

Maybe Because

I don't know why I only write about love,
But maybe it's because the darkness in this world is too much I want to light it up with this love.
Maybe because I have been bruised, called, named, shamed but never loved,
Maybe because I know it feels different from what they gave me,
Maybe because I am still searching.
I don't know why I only write about love,
But maybe it's because the love in this world is drowning.
Maybe because you hate me, I hate you and they hate each other but you love him,
Maybe because I have too much love from never knowing what love is,
Maybe because I am trying to wrap up evil in love and tell the world to forget,
Maybe because love is so unreal I talk about shit love and still love the shit love gives me,
I don't know why I only write about love,
But maybe it's because I have been through painful love I only breathe pernicious love,
Maybe because I cannot feel it and now I imagine what it would feel like,
Maybe because what I write is more beautiful than what they could give,
Maybe because I have been broken, hurt, cut, split, lit; all in the name of love,
Maybe because I have told myself I can heal through the love inked on my paper,
Maybe because I smile memories, paint words, dance to letters, sing air, fall in you and love nothing
But then again . . .
Maybe it's because I love.

Tatenda Mushayi

Love Of My Life

I can't resist,
Your touch,
I'm in bliss,
So much.

My love,
But a kiss,
Looked on from up above,
You I would surely miss.

Jonathan Simms

Love Doesn't Live Here Anymore

Love doesn't live here anymore
Only pulling of my heart strings,
And the closing of the door.
Empty vases
Flowers all around have died,
Tears a-falling
Only empty cries inside.
Love has gone
From this heart of mine,
Someone I was in love with
I thought would love me in time.
He walked out that door
He said to me!
'I don't love you anymore,
I've gone back with someone,
That I was in love with before!'
No arms wrapped around me
No arms to hold me tight,
No one to say anymore
'I'll love you always and goodnight!'

Sweet dreams
Are a thing of the past
Only heartaches and pain
'How long will it last!'
No more butterflies in the stomach
No more buzzing of the bees,
No more honey do I taste
No more flowers do I smell,
Or the weakness of the knees.
No more kisses do you send
On a carpet of blossoms to me,
'Why did you walk through that door?'
Telling me that you wanted to be free.
The colours that you bought
With the warmth from your soul,
As left me now with darkness
Angry and cold.
'I loved you!'

Mary Woolvin

REGRETS

I said goodbye to my dearest love,
It would be a task I'd not want to repeat;
I should have put my arms around him,
But the future for me, then hit so bleak . . .

I regret those few precious moments,
When I should have spoken of my love;
But my thoughts were filled with dread,
That I'd be here, and he in Heaven above . . .

We'd spent so many years together,
I knew nought of life without him;
From schoolgirl into marriage,
When we'd happily sink or swim . . .

My life seems oh so empty now,
Yes, I've friends who help me through;
But really all I need in my life,
Is to be back safe, and loved by you . . .

I miss our love much more than I,
Could ever realize on that last day;
And much more how I should have
Opened my mouth, to truly say . . .

That no one can ever take your place,
Of the two of us together, as one;
For that seemed always destined,
But it's so hard now that you're gone . . .

I have no choice but to venture on,
Until I reach Heaven, and you;
To hold me, and to pull me close,
Where once again, we can become two . . .

Janet Starkey

When You Get Home

Last night lying in your arms felt right
Blood pumping and heart so tight
Couldn't sleep – the clock said two
Kissed your cheek – whispered – love you
Wanting so much to make this our home.

Woke up this morning when you had gone
Turned on the radio – heard our song
Reminded me of times gone past
Made me sure that we would last
Dinner on the table when you . . . get home

Baby, baby we were oh so meant to be
The only word that goes with you is me
We were just oh so so meant to be
There is no end to the magic together
That we can make . . .
When you . . .
Get home

Picked your washing up off the floor
Hung your dressing gown on the door
Smelling the pillow where you lay
Thinking of last night throughout the day
Looking forward to when you call this . . . home

You've been badly hurt and so have I
Let's take a huge leap of faith and try
It takes two to tango but one to ask
Say yes and years later we could bask
In memories of the time we called this home

Baby, baby we were oh so meant to be
The only word that goes with you is me
We were just oh so so meant to be
There is no end to the magic together
That we can make . . .
When you . . .
Get home

Should we take the risk after all that's gone before
We both did so much to raise up off the floor
Do you want to go back to a house or rush back home
Loneliness or my voice as the ringtone on your phone
Let's take the risk and open up the door
To our home

Last night lying in your arms felt right

Blood pumping and heart so tight
Woke up and the clock said two
Kissed your cheek – whispered - love you
Wanting so much to make this our home

Baby, baby we were oh so meant to be
The only word that goes with you is me
We were just oh so so meant to be
There is no end to the magic together
That we can make . ..
When you . . .
Get home

There is no end to the magic together
That we can make . . .
When you . . .
Get home.

Warren Kemp

Changing Face Of Romance

Roses and kisses
Romantic ideal
No Valentine misses
As lovers appeal

But will they then lose it
Leave each other forlorn?
Passion a brief hit
As vows are then torn?

Flowing time tells us
That after a spell
Lovers, they will cuss
As all fails to gel.

Tracy Allott

My Love Letter

Dear Lover
You'd be my life if I ever had one,
You'd be my soul to keep me in check,
You stand afore me to watch the rising sun,
But I will stand with you always.

Without you poetry has no meaning,
The words I have no rhyme,
The tower of Pisa would not be leaning,
If paper had no lines.

You gaze upon me with eyes of blue,
The deeper meaning within your heart,
Yet love would never stay true,
If we ended with the start.

You wouldn't be human if you didn't confess mistakes,
Don't quote poetry for you're wasting your time,
Every word sounds fake,
And I already know that you are mine.

If you can prove you're happy with my smile,
Then Shakespeare will have proven love,
That you cannot buy this smile,
But you can buy a turtle dove.

I guess my metaphors have fallen flat,
It's easier to write what I would say,
Only your heart is big and fat,
I will love you every day.

Charlotte O'Farrell

Her Eyes

Her eyes revive me more than God's blue sea,
Her smile is more radiant than spring's day.
To think on her doth fill me up with glee,
Doth calm me more than a tropical bay.
What would she say if I told her my dreams?
If I told her my mind and spoke my heart?
The feelings of a heart burned by moonbeams,
Now pierced and fixed by Cupid's sweet dart.
O Lord above! If Thou art existent,
If You would permit me to have her love,
To be loved by she who seemed so distant,
My heart would soar to the Heavens above.
Let me swim in the ocean of her eyes;
Free me from the sound of these Devil's cries!

William Green

Quicksand

Your love attacks like quicksand,
Homing in on every side.
No matter where I run to,
I cannot stem its tide.

I'm afraid it's all consuming
And clearly has my measure.
No matter my resistance,
It remains a guilty pleasure.

Oh yes, you're pure quicksand,
Sucking me right in.
Clinging to me every day,
Like a second skin.

Paul Kelly

Her Lace Left With Me

'Twas twilight's rain in a beauteous land
When all the birds and flowers were to sleep,
Yet the stars had unveiled themselves to peep
At Romeo holding his Juliet's hand.
'My heart has been forever lost in thine
And it can ask for no greater a bliss
Than for thee dear to be forever mine.'
How could Juliet such true love decline?
She answered Romeo with a vowing kiss.

Thereafter, flitted she off in delight
Not before promising to come back soon;
And Romeo, gazing at the silver moon,
Had eyes that thirsted for his Juliet's sight.
And as he longed for her, his heart had felt
His Juliet's presence from a place around;
He went about to search and when he knelt,
His heart too with delight did heavenly melt,
For it was Juliet's lace that he had found.

Romeo then followed Juliet – in his mind
A thought of holding close his love again,
But he received imperishable pain,
For he saw what he never thought he'd find:
'Twas Juliet that he saw in ravishing beauty,
In the arms of 'nother she did prevail.
Taking on poor Romeo no pious pity,
Juliet cried tears in felicity;
And Romeo cried tears in unsought betrayal.

That night was fraught with rueful mourning cries
And every leaf now knew of Romeo how
No heart did throb in his irksome chest now
And no life ever danced in his cold eyes.
He could live not nor die; not love nor hate
In the time that moved slowly every day
With Juliet's lace reminding him his fate:
Romeo – a lover flower fore'er in wait,
Juliet – a butterfly flown away.

'Tis twilight's rain in a beauteous land
When all the birds and flowers are to sleep,
Yet the stars have unveiled themselves to peep
At Romeo, holding Juliet's lace in hand.
The lace with two ends is kept very neat.
For one end shows him his Juliet's glee
And th'other shows him Juliet's deceit;
'The one did always with the other meet,'
Writes Romeo in his 'Her Lace Left With Me'.

Hassan Imran

ANGEL

When I woke up this morning and I saw you lying there
With the sunlight through the curtains shining in your hair,
I looked at you lovingly, while you lay asleep
Then leaned over to kiss you gently on your cheek.
And I do believe it's true to say
I think I have kissed an Angel today.

We sat together at the breakfast table, with talk of the day ahead
As always you had something to say, to help me clear my head.
The phone rang, one of the children, needing you again
You patiently talked and listened to her, taking away her pain.
And I do believe it's true to say
I think I have spoken to an Angel today.

When I came home in the evening, at the end of a busy day,
You were there at the door to meet me, in your usual way.
I'd never seen you more beautiful, in the clothes you wear
I held you close to kiss you, while my hand ran through your hair.
And I do believe it's true to say
I think I have seen an Angel today.

Now as I lay beside you, as you sleep, in the dark of the night
I think how you always bring to my life, so much love and light.
Without your love I would be, like a candle without a flame,
For the close ones, who share our love, it would be the same.
And I do believe it's true to say
I think I have loved an Angel today.

Tim Kitchen

HOMESICK

Far.
It is not long since the moon crept in
And broke a few silver paces across the deck.
Not far
Since the light held your eyes,
As a lonely crystal flew
Across your face.
Liquid.

It is not far.
Since the day waved goodbye to morning
Welcoming politely the afternoon.
It is not far,
Since the Earth jumped to caress you,
Warm its kiss upon your face encased in nevers and not evers.
It is not far
To walk to hear your laughter.
No,
It is not far.

Natalie Williams

CUPID'S TART

Years have come and years have gone
Through them all our love's grown strong.
Fate entwined our paths to cross
It was my gain, but sadly another girl's loss!
We've travelled afar, shared 'once in a lifetime' moments,
Stayed in top luxury hotels; camped in two man tents.
We sometimes quarrel over minor issues –
Toilet seats, football, handbags and shoes!
Our love has produced two beautiful girls,
A gift from God, our legacy in the world.
When I look into your eyes I still melt within,
I'm that girl by the flexi clock but in older skin!
I kiss your lips and stroke your hair,
I think of our future and know nothing matters as long as you're there.
Only I hold the secret key to unlock your heart,
Your eyes smoulder with desire as I offer my homemade apple tart!

Carole Dickinson

ASPECTS OF LOVE

They say love changes everything
And this we know is true
I never felt this way before
The day that I met you
My heart it turned a somersault
I felt I was in Heaven
When slowly you walked up to me
That day in sunny Devon
I saw the warmth emitting
From your gorgeous hazel eyes
And I wanted to embrace you
As you brushed against my thighs
I knew it was no accident
That we had come together
It was decreed there in the stars
Our love would last for ever.

Elizabeth Green

JAFFA CAKES

My friend,
Take my hand and come with me
Let's eat lunch by the apple tree
And if your smile is not fake
I'll give you my Jaffa Cake.
My lover,
Take me by the hips
Soothe me with your gentle lips
And if your love makes my heart quake
I'll let you lick my Jaffa Cake.
My beloved,
Take me to be your wedded wife
Stay with me all your life
And if you keep the vows you make
I'll cook you a Jaffa Cake.
My husband,
Take my arm and sit
To watch our children play a bit
Love is give, and love is take
I'll share with you my Jaffa Cake.

Heather Harwood

My Valentine

The ring on my third left finger
Reminds me every single day
Of the vows we made to each other
To love each other come what may
There's good and bad in all of us
We've had our share it's true
But I hope the day will never come
When I can't stand by you
We've been through good and bad times
We've aged with the seasons and time
We've laid and stood together
It hasn't always been sublime
Now we're old and still together
We adhered through the thick and the thin
Both adjusted with no trepidation
As our autumn of lives does begin
So when all those younger lovers
Think only they can feel so fine
They've yet to savour our true sweet love
My sweetheart, my eternal Valentine.

Cedric A Thrupp

You're My . . .

You're my breath I take to keep alive,
You're my shadow that is by my side,
You're the sun that warms up my face,
You're the sweetness in my favourite cake,
You're my heart that beats in my chest,
You're the perfect place to lay my head,
You're my earth, water, wind and fire,
You're everything I want and desire,
You're everything to me and always will,
With you by my side my life is fulfilled.

Emma McNamara

LOVE TEETH

I cried at the dentist
After five milk teeth;
The age I was at.
No one to kiss the tears goodbye.

I cried at the loneliness of
my first day at school,
St Maggie's; the Thatcherite years.
No one to kiss my tears goodbye.

I cried at the age of fifteen.
I didn't know why.
I just had to cry.
No one to kiss the tears goodbye.

I didn't cry at the age of twenty.
But twenty petals did that for me.
No one to kiss the tears goodbye.

I cried at the age of twenty five,
when that same dentist pulled out a wisdom.
Someone came to kiss away the pain,
but no one to kiss the tears goodbye.

Rachel Van Den Bergen

THE OWL AND THE PUSSYCAT

A lawnmower shaves away another busy week
Leaving the garden awash with a fresh new aftershave,
And in that quiet light, reason and rhyme find some time
To smile away the usual nonsense of another busy day
Before settling down, cuddling in, and . . . whatever . . .

Robert Black

Silent Word Poetry

His hand was his comfort,
His voice and his grace,
Chanting silent word poetry,
As he stroked my face.

I didn't need to see him,
Just simply loved his touch,
His rhyming was my reason,
My eyes, I kept them shut.

Every word I understood,
And I breathed in every sound,
A sonnet that embraced my heart,
My soul, my mind, spellbound.

I never knew quite what he meant,
But I knew what I had heard,
A quiet opera to cleanse my heat,
A soliloquy of silent words.

Kayt Pritchard

Along The Promenade

We walk hand in hand as the dusk softly falls
And the light lends the landscape a luminous glow.
How the calendar pages have fallen away
Since our young selves first came here in days long ago.
Proud new parents we strolled in our bubble of joy,
With our babe snugly wrapped against early spring chills.
Such a closeness engulfed us as, nestling in love,
We watched silver tipped clouds over mist shadowed hills.

Now our babe is a wife with two babes of her own,
So long and so short seems the progress of years.
Her happiness fuels the stove of our love
Which has burnt strong and steady through triumph and fears.
With your warm hand in mine as we walk by the bay,
The lifetime of caring, which made us as one,
Continues and strengthens and binds us together
For each precious moment our Sands of Time run.

Ann Warren

Growing Pains

Oh! I do *so* want a Valentine, I'm wishing really hard,
That someone out there likes me enough to send a card.
He doesn't have to *love* me, or be soppy, or be – Yuk!
Or send me lots of roses, just a card to wish me luck.

I'm sure my friends at school will have at *least* one card apiece
Even the ugly, spotty ones and those that are obese.
I'm sitting on the staircase with my backpack on my knee,
And praying that the post will bring an envelope for me.

Otherwise I really do not want to go to school,
Unless I have a Valentine I really won't be cool.
I wonder if I'm stupid to think that he might care
He probably doesn't even know that I am there.

I thought the looks he gave me were meaningful and shy
His soulful eyes at dinnertime, while eating shepherd's pie,
Made me go quite trembly, I had to dash away,
I wasn't very hungry so I didn't need to stay.

Was it just by chance that we met up at the fair
Did he know that I was going? Did he know that I'd be there?
In the noisy bumper car we touched all down my thigh
Of course, it could be gravity that made me want to fly.

It isn't much to go on, I wish that there was more.
Ah, there's the postman's whistle, he's coming to our door.
An ad for double-glazing, and a bill falls on the ground
My heart drops to my trainers, then leaps back with a bound

A stiff white envelope, of satisfying size,
Lies squarely on the doormat, I can't believe my eyes!
Addressed to 'Janice Cartwright' I hug it to my chest,
This Valentine's my first, my longed for and my best!

Margaret Pace

WHAT YOU ARE

You are the wintry sun
That shines like a pearl
Through silvery slates of sky

You are the ruffles of sunset
That dance like roses
On ripples of river

You are a motionless drop of moment
In the rushing tide of time.

You are the first diamond
In the velvet blanket
Of darkening dusk

You are the iridescent dawn
That paints the frame
For the winter willow silhouette

You are the genuine smile
In the posed photograph.

You are the azure loch
Hidden in folds
Of untouched valley

You are the tiny church,
From times past,
Nestled between skyscraper and hotel

You are the unseen band of gold
Around my fumbling finger.

You are the single feather
That floats through air,
Touching head, after foot, after hand

You are the drops of dew
That makes the web
Beautiful.

You are the pen
That writes my words.

You are the sanity
In a whirling cyclone
Of confusion

You are the flower
That blossoms
In the patch of weeds

You are the fire that fuels
My imagination

You are the candlelight
That flickers on the wall
And casts a thousand dreams

You are the inspiration
For every thought, word
And smile

You are the opposite of McGough's
What you are

You are the answer
And I am the question.

Caroline Jones

Unrequited Love

Did you hear me call my love, high up
In your ivory tower?
Thought you my cry a happy one, or
Just a trifle sour.
Had you someone with you, when ere I
Came to call?
Did I see two shadows, there upon your wall.

What have I done my dearest, that you no
Longer hear?
My cry of pain and anguish; sighs and
Bitter tears.
Pray tell me quick that I may find, the
Love within your heart,
I cannot bear this life to live, if you
And I should part.

The sky would lose its glory, the sun its
Warm embrace,
No longer could I endure this world,
Without your dear, sweet face.
Though many have your lovers been, I swear
I love but you,
Pray leave me not my darling, for my poor
Love is true.

Peter Mahoney

EACH OTHER

The hot, sweet bacon spits
Its smoky morning call,
The pearly wisps of scent
Flirt past the smoke alarm
Before curling up inside their nostrils.

Their stomachs are the first to wake
Exchanging polite, gargling greetings
Then their muscles begin to follow
Twitching, flexing
A well-practised routine.

They wander idly through a catalogue
Of fresh dreams; soon to be forgotten
Probing for sense.
They trace the miles of open mattress with their fingertips
Searching for each other.

A magnetic puppet master
Draws the delicate hairs that line her back
To twine themselves around
Their counterparts
That fleck his stomach.

He strokes the smooth fold on her ear
Knowing it's always been there
But now he knows it's his secret
She hides it
Behind her hair.

Their hot skin sparks as they turn blindly towards each other
Their eyes flicker heavily open
She traces every shadow on his pillow-pressed face.

She smiles.
It is now morning.

Natalie Moores

My Story

In early teens we met each other
Her from the typing pool and became my lover.
Our first date was to a football match with 15,000 others
We would get on our bikes and say farewell to our mothers.

To the countryside we would ride
With trusted camera by our side,
We snapped this and that our love never died
Criticism of older people deigned

As time went on we tied the knot
April in Paris is what we got,
The honeymoon was very hot
Memories are precious, I kid you not.

Years move on, we've now notched up fifty seven
Tell you young folks it's like living in Heaven,
There's three children, six grandchildren, no chance of seven?
Time has just gone by we are fortunate to have been given.

Years have flown by and it's been a struggle
People might think we are now in a muddle,
Now time is of the essence we can still love and cuddle
In spite of hip problems, diabetes, stroke, cataracts, it's a struggle.

Of Valentine's days, we have experienced many
In future years there may be some then again there could not be any,
Excuses for divorce are two a penny
Now my heartburn's playing up I must have a Rennie.

John Waby

First Love

A hug in the school canteen
Thick sturdy coat, bright green
Two pint glasses left at the bar
And then it's up the road, not too far

The disc spins on the turntable
Round and round, fact not fable
We muse on times present and times past
We get on with each other fast

I am careless and clumsy
The needle of the arm of the record player jumps a groove
He goes back to his mates and another room
And I have never seen his dustpan and broom.

Ann Barefoot

In Love

In perfumed anticipation
Rustling guests and relations wait
Peeking under whispering brims
In best dressed creations and trims.
Footsteps falter under preludes
While best men press pockets bemused.
Announcing chords swell under arches
As bride and father step to marches.
Glances catch the blush and light of eye.
Mothers feel the touch of time and cry
Honeyed bridesmaids with pert noses
Clutch long veils and tender posies.
Before priest and people side by side
Bridegroom steals looks from chosen bride.
Vows are ringed and sealed with tender kiss
Sign of faith in future happiness.
Petalled processions lead the way
As smiles and hands enfold the day.

Shirley Johnson

Ocean My Love

Her beauty makes me want to cry
I know that one day she will fly

To make her home with a loving man
I always want to hold her hand

So lovely and pure she's 12-years-old
Big brown eyes and hair of gold

Thoughtful, fun caring and true,
At home with me she cuddles and grew

Out into this world full and bright
Wishing to never let her out of my sight

The angels will look down on her for me,
Protect her from dangers she may not see

Like an invisible veil to keep the bad out,
Protecting her own, I have no doubt

Mama's pasta or perhaps some roast beef?
My time with her seems ever so brief.

She used to be allergic to chocolate, no milk,
Her skin will be smooth, it will be like silk

Her body is growing the reluctance is there
Her favourite is Oliver, loving trusted bear.

She hand made a cushion, a project at school
If she is sick I tend to her keeping it cool.

She never lies still, when asleep in my bed,
Most redeeming quality, is her thoughtful head

Dances around to music that she likes,
Up mountains and hills she likes to hike

Up a tree or in a river that tickles her toes
I know what you remember her Mama knows

Ocean I'm so proud of you, my love is so strong
I could shout from a rooftop or bang on a gong.

Mama x

Meia Alegranza

True For Evermore

The first time ever I fell in love, I really lost my heart
To Josephine, the girl next door, so elegant, so smart.
But my romance was doomed to failure from the very start,
Cos she was twelve, and I was only four!
But youthful broken hearts soon mend, and schooldays helped a lot,
Cos I discovered Ann, and all my schoolwork went to pot:
The seventh birthday kiss she gave me made me go all hot
And I sword I'd be true for evermore.

When I was nine, sweet Madeline made Ann a memory,
Those cherry lips, those big blue eyes, they did strange things to me,
But soon, she found someone who had a better bike than me,
I'd never fall in love again, I sword!
And 'til the ripe old age of twelve, I celibate remained,
Until Odette, the PE Mistress, got me all inflamed.
To worship her, I did PE until I felt quite drained.
And I swore I'd be true for evermore.

Then Marion came on the scene, and made my senses quiver,
I loved her so, that there was not a thing I wouldn't give her.
But after showering her with gifts, I realized with a shiver,
That she was playing games with me for sure!
But then I noticed Jennifer, I followed her from school,
She let me take her dancing at the local Co-op hall
And as we shuffled round, I knew that once again I'd fall,
And swear that I'd be true for evermore.

On holiday that year, I met with Carol! Tasty? Whew!
And Jenny, left behind, was soon replaced by passions new,
They say romance on holidays can't last, but that's untrue,
Our romance lasted seven weeks or more!
But when I first set eyes on Eileen, did my senses reel,
Such feelings she aroused in me, I never thought I'd feel,
Instinctively I knew that this was love, and love for real,
And I swore I'd be true for evermore.

And true I was until next summer, when I met sweet Jean,
As sensual a siren as my eyes have ever seen,
She led me into idylls where I'd never ever been,
But disappeared when I went back for more!
But Carol was on hand to stop the pain within my heart,
She was so blonde, so beautiful, so shapely, so smart,
She told me that she loved me and we'd never ever part,
And I swore I'd be true for evermore.

Now Carol had a friend called Christine, she was something rare,

ASPECTS OF *Love* - A Collection Of Poetry

She showed me some pastimes that a boy and girl could share,
But Carol caught us passing time once when she wasn't there,
And didn't want to know me any more.
I pined and pined for both of them 'til Linda came along,
And once again, at seventeen, my heart was full of song,
This romance would last for ever, nothing would go wrong,
And I swore I'd be true for evermore.

Two weeks later, Lin had gone off with another fella,
But Carol-3 came by, if Lin was sell, then she was sweller,
But she was flash, and I was shy, and too tongue-tied to tell her,
So there I was, back on the shelf once more,
'Til Marie slinked along and I just stared at her aghast,
She really was a looker, and I soon forgot the past,
For those who'd gone before were crushes, this was 'it' at last,
And I sword I'd be true for evermore.

'It' lasted just a week, I cried, then Diane dried my tears,
She told me that she loved me and our love would last for years,
But then her waistline grew, and it confirmed my silent fears,
That someone else had 'been there' just before,
But shortly after, at a wedding, I caught Susan's eye,
She laid her head upon my shoulder, gave a gentle sigh,
And when I told her how I felt, I knew it was no lie,
And I swore I'd be true for evermore.

But Sue lived far away, while Angela lived much more close,
And Angie swore that she'd be mine 'Until Hell's fire froze'
It must have been the coldest winter ever, I suppose,
It wasn't long before I knew the score,
But Jenny, who I worked with, cast a sideways glance at me,
I'd never realized just how tasty one's workmates could be,
So taking both her hands in mine, I smiled lovingly,
And I swore I'd be true for evermore.

It came as a surprise to find that Jen was spoken for,
I really felt depressed, dejected, slighted, and unsure,
Until I met another Carol (Carol number four),
And both my feet were three feet from the floor,
And so, in nineteen-sixty-six, my 'hunting day's were through,
I walked her down the aisle and we said the words, 'I do.'
And there, before an eager crowd of everyone we knew,
I swore I would be true for evermore.

Mick Nash

Endless Love

Waiting too long
Wishing she would turn back
Regretting saying goodbye
His heart stopped beating the moment she turned away
And never came back

It's been ten years
Yet he still waits
Day and night
For the person he loved
No matter what weather

Does he not know
It's been ten long years
And he no longer lives
He is now just a ghost waiting
His love's return
Frozen by the cold winter's snow
He continuous waiting . . .
In the winter wonderland where they first met.

Rita Mateus

Soulmates

When you're here with me
I feel you touching every part of me.
I hear you say my name
With every breath you take.
We belong together . . .

It's called fate.

I saw you first amongst
The guise of a crowd.
You blew me away
With your beautiful smile,
That reached your gorgeous big blue eyes.

You are the only one –
Forever more . . .

Jagdeesh Sokhal

What Is Love

Love is the night, love is the day
Love so so near, love so far away
Love makes you smile, love brings a tear to the eye
Love lifts you so high, love can make you cry

Love sends you into raptures, every day
Love it sends you to places where, no one can say
Your feet do not touch, do not touch the ground
Words of love, truly a wonderful sound

But love it sends your heart, high into space
It looks at you, it just adores your face
That moment will send you, into a wonderful dream
So so alive, you must create a scene

Your heart skips so many beats, it doesn't feel right
Relax smile, you truly are in Heaven's sight
Love raises you up so high, love holds you tight
Love makes you smile, love keeps you awake at night

Love is that feeling that cannot be tamed
Love takes your life, you'll never be the same
Love in your heart, morning, noon and night
Love that precious candle, that burns so bright

Love is the stars, the moon, the sun
Love is the past, and the future to come
Love has no number, love makes your heart shiver
Love makes you believe in today, makes you believe in forever

So keep a place in your heart, for that love to come
Remember love, asks no questions of anyone
Love is never ending, love never dies
Love is life love is truth, I hear you cry.

So let love into your heart, don't be shy
What greater words, can you hear him cry
I love you with all my heart, you know this is true
What other man could love you, love you like I do

So let that love that is within be there for all
Open your heart enjoy life, have a ball
For love is life and love is truth
Your presence here, is the living proof.

Allan Brebner

THE CIRCLE OF LOVE

Love is a mother's tender hand which dries
Salty tears from her children's cheeks and eyes.

Love is a kiss on a child's feverish brow,
With mother softly whispering, 'hush now.'

Love is happy innocent youngsters at play,
Should we understand what they're saying?

Love is the twinkling smile between
Friends observing a magical scene.

Love is the warmth and pleasure of clasped hands
As a couple strolls along golden sands.

Love is two swollen hearts beating together
In unison – light as a bird's feather.

Love is as sweet as the scent of roses
Just at the precise moment he proposes.

Love is memories of a life
Spent together as husband and wife.

Love crosses numerous divides:
We never know where it resides.

Patricia J Tausz

I WROTE YOUR NAME IN CRYSTAL WATERS

I wrote our name in crystal waters
Each letter drowned before the next
Your name lost in forgotten dreams
But I recalled your gentle smile
Your dimpled cheeks your lips so red
You laughed and the world was free at peace
The wind sang to you amongst the leaves
I wrote your name in crystal waters
I lost you to the world's embrace
Your name lost in forgotten dreams
The song of the wind amongst the leaves
. . . Was lost to me
I wrote your name in crystal waters.

David M Walford

Aspects Of Love

What a difference a day makes,
Through my window,
All things return,
In all its colourful wonder,
I am amazed by change.
In the weather and fate,

Don't hesitate to understand,
In all of us, we are one,
In one second, we are strong,
Turning on the stations,
To please the senses,
No longer blind,

The past has come across,
And seen into the future,
It is surreal, to waste this space,
Made to last light years,
One second to live the dream,
One lifetime to learn within.

Chris Watts

Clinging To The Drift

As we stalked the rein of humble fields,
Walking with dogs, as mystery took hold.
Forests dusted the ground with their yields,
Catching with the speed of a common cold.

Much like wild dogs ourselves in many ways,
From the titillating embrace you lent.
Embarking from a train through a heaped haze,
To the simplest glace at a chance event.

You are the one, always holding my heart.
Even the sea I crossed was all for you.
Though I did not know it would kill the art.
From first to last it was me chasing you.

And if it were you who abandoned ship,
Why am I the one clinging to the drift?

David Chrzanowski

Seeing You Again

I was not there
You were not here
But let's be clear
Seeing you again
Evoked old feelings
I still care
I will do for years
But it's different now
Easier somehow
Than I thought
It would be
We talked
We laughed
Stayed up late
And I can't wait
To see you again
Now I know
We can be friends.

Andrew Fisher

Sheet Whispers

The sheet of my heart upon the paper masks the loveless empty sheets of my bed
Without lover or sweet prose between the folds of my heart
Seldom is the binding spirit that etches itself upon my lonely soul
Lost somewhere between the blank wood of the trees and the sheets of paper
Which foretells of stories of lost love which echoes and resonates in my wooden framed bed
And is lost within a passionless night.
The nights of longing and ink soaked thoughts upon I lay my solitude my, mortal frame.
The ink of a lost love is forever stained upon the empty sheets upon which I lay which mirrors the empty sheets of paper with no sweet words written upon them as though they are whispered so gently
Upon the paper as if reminiscent of sweet words left unspoken between two lovers.

Serita Blake

The Moody Moo And The Mizog*

A cranky old goat,
Mizog grumbled and groaned
and greeted most others with growls
(he had a sweet smile
but it was more his style
to stifle it
with bitter scowls).

A Moody Moo
crossed his path one day,
moping, she moaned and she mumbled
(her eyes were a treat
if yours they should meet
but she kept them downturned
– still she stumbled!)

Now Mizog might grouch
but sure couldn't bear
to see another in pain –
he rushed to her side,
her eyes opened wide
and his smile
touched her more than her sprain.

(* a Mizog is a miserable old git)

Jackie Joseph

Unguarded Heart

My heart,
Like the one I see before me, in my hot chocolate cup, all swirly, frothed, melted.
The shape of a heart on the surface.
Underneath a cauldron of desire, like chilli chocolate.
Once attached, I never thought I would feel love's keen sting again.
How could I be so stupid to leave my heart unguarded?

Yazmin White

NOVEMBER DAYS

I can remember the time I first loved you
I was sitting in a coffee shop, staring out the window
Thinking thoughts that . . .
If I think about them now
I can't even recall what they were But you, I remember you
Walking past the window on that cold November day
You looked different from the rest of the crowd
Like you were from a foreign place
Making up your mind your hand touched the door
The same hand you now place on my lower back
A silent promise that you will always be close by
I shouldn't have stared, I know that now
But I could not take my eyes off you
You were a welcome distraction
To what had been a dismal day
You placed your order, it was the same as mine
Even down to the paper cup
It was crowded in the coffee shop
On that cold November day
The one empty seat was next to mine
And I was willing the Gods
That you would sit by my side
My prayers were answered
As you rested your weary legs
And it felt the angels in Heaven
Were rejoicing above my head
'Cheer up,' you said
'It can't be that bad'
'You'd be surprised' came the reply
'Some people find it easier talking to a stranger,
Why not give it a try.'
So to the stranger with these gentle hands
And the slight accent to his voice
I told him my story
I don't know why, but the floodgates opened
He never interrupted me the whole time
All he did was all I wanted, he simply listened
When I had finished he gave me advice
Which I later put to good use
I then asked him where he was from
He confirmed that he was from the Med
Which explained the accent, the tan
And his lovely dark eyes and hair

One hour passed and then two
It was time for me to leave
'I know it sounds strange,' the man said
'But it feels like I've known you forever.'
I had to admit that this bond felt strange
And I was willing to pursue it further
So after swapping our numbers and our names
We left the shop together
We kept in touch and time passed by
And I now realize one thing
That on that dark, cold November day
I found my true love and my soulmate.

Lisa Burton

Moment Of Peace

Here dappled shadows fall across a stream
Where first we met so many years ago
And still the ageing heart recalls a glow
Like winter sun that melts December snow
Of joy that might have been.

In me no hunger now, in me no pain
As one short day fades to mysterious night
And flaring stars are luminously bright
You come to me ethereal and light,
Moment of peace remain.

A river mist forms and divides to trace
Her ghostly magic here, a water-sprite
That has no lodging found to spend the night
And by the hour of daybreak must take flight
From this enchanted place.

A world apart, the air perfumed with flowers,
Musk intermingled with the pale dog rose,
Beneath, as clear as glass the river flows,
Her lonely way only the otter knows
And that this once was ours.

Frances M Searle

The Stars

The stars
Beloved gave your mouth to me
The dark
Unveiled lights that kindled our kiss

Between
Our lips first spark mingled into flame
Breathe into me
As I breathe into you; waves

Wash over me
Sweet your kisses, you searched
Out all my secrets;
Waves flood through me

So you kissed me
Beneath world and line moved
Through me; energy soared,
Pleasure swept into me

Your soul would kiss me
As world unfolds gold
I hold quietness of waiting within me.

Our lips will meet again.

Teresa Webster

Valentine

V alentine, will you be mine
A lways, every day?
L oving, caring, giving, serving
E ach and every hour.
N ever straying from the vows we made,
T hinking only of the best,
I n sickness and in health together,
N ow and for
E ver, precious Valentine!

Cathy Mearman

NEW LOVE

As new and green,
My love and yours,
It went along
And by the hazel grove,
As underneath the curving wood
We walked,
With little heed of time
That is forever moving
In the trackless land.
Oh, may this one blue, careless day
Be ours,
To love and laugh
And speak our name,
And sip the cup of paradise.

Harry Stevenson

MY SUN

Warm in your embrace, cold air circles us,
Life is filled with fear and uncertainty,
Somber thoughts swept away by power of trust,
Trapped inside my mind, you make me feel free.

A sad bird whose essence has been clipped,
Potential energy escapes from me.
A moth whose flame has been extinguished,
The heat of life is squandered easily.

Once upon a time in a land far away,
Roses, castles, spinning in the night.
Our future ahead of us, on display.
Help me to find a way back to the light.

For you alone are the only one,
For you alone can reignite my sun.

Laura Muskin

Find Me In A Dream

I never thought you'd leave me –
Didn't think I'd see you go,
You walked away so calmly –
How could you treat me so . . . ?

Oh, how the memory grieves me –
Of how you went your way.
The years of great illusions
Were shattered in a day . . .

A day of sad regretment,
Of all the might have beens,
If I'd have known your longings
To place them in your dreams . . .

You didn't leave a message
Of where I went so wrong,
Just left a deep dark sorrow
And nights that seem so long . . .

My days are all so empty –
Keep thinking thoughts so blue.
No good in having plenty
Of love if I've not you . . .

So think again, my darling,
Of how it could have been;
And maybe if I'm lucky –
You'll find me in a dream . . .

Echo:
You'll find me in a dream –
Please find me in a dream!
- Think on me in your dream,
And all that might have been . . .

Mary Pauline Winter, nee Coleman

The Third Man

Now the time has come to finally part
Do you go home to Mother with your broken heart?
There's one thing, she can't say 'I told you so.'
It's a secret she isn't supposed to know.
Men don't advertise loving each other
Still unacceptable. Kept under cover
By creating girlfriends,
Love children, sordid past.
Love between two men?
– That was never meant to be.

There's no longer two of you, now there's three.
The hurt he's caused he pretends not to see.
Doesn't want to come between you or cause a row
The lying bastard! Explains to you how
We could share the same flat, and get along great,
You look on him not as a thief, but a mate.
You get a quick peek of himself in the buff,
His way of being friendly, bonding stuff.
The fool thinks love's battles are over, he's won.
You could warn him, his have not even begun.

Your bags are packed, love affair at an end.
You tell them you're spending the night with a friend.
Smile as you say your last goodbye,
Don't let them see the tear in your eye.
You hand over the keys and open the door,
Yet would give the whole world for just one night more
In his arms to try to hold onto his love,
But it's futile, and now that you've made your move
You see that the lies and deceit all began
When you entered his life – and you were 'third man'.

Mike Silkstone

My Love Dilemma

To repress my heart, but how long for?
I feel I have to close the door.
One person I crave to be my soulmate forever with me.
Who so perfectly matched –
We would never fight, never disagree.
Remain eternally happy.
But, choice has made it not so.
I'm unsure of which road to go.
She offers me youth and hunger for life,
do I choose her and make her my wife?
Or go with the old flame, whose candle slowly burns out,
I'm a hopeless dreamer, with a restless spirit,
but I need your wings to yield me and shield me,
Love me, hold me, be my one human soul who I can trust dearly.
Love me in spite of my faults, guide me with thy knowledge.
Can you offer me this? I ask myself, yet undecided I stand.
The voice of reason or heart in my hand.
I suppress the heart and go with the reason of choice,
The offer is a challenge, and a journey through reason of voice . . .

Nicola Jean Holden

Love Did Not Find Me

Love did not find me under moonlit skies,
adorned with silver stars and crystal sprays;
nor on the airy strains of symphonies,
nor in the heady heat of summer days.

It came upon me softly, through a pall
of broken dreams; when I had had my fill
of love and lies. Determined not to fall
I let it lie, though it would find me still.

But now I see through time's slow clarity;
those agonies were but the overtures
in love's great symphony. And self pity
is not justified when fonder love endures.

Such flames were but the fire that purifies;
brief portents of the flame that never dies.

Steve Waterfield

Untitled

Oh Valentine with heart of stone
No marrow, marble in your bone.
With wistful eye I gaze at thee
But you're too cold to notice me.
And so I stay alone.

What wishful thoughts inside my head
As you repose each night in bed?
Not charity, or grace, I trow
For these are foreign thoughts to thou.
All love for me but dead.

Virtue, innocence, fidelity, will ne'er be known again.
Love's oaths lie in the field dead – slain.
My heart in pain, and pain there be.
Your tarnished promise in memory,
Washed pure by gentle rain.

Oh Valentine, stay well away!
Close thine ears to what I say.
Live on in ignorant belief,
My love will bring thee no relief,
I'll stop loving thee – some day.

Jim Ryder

An Idyll Of Love

The softest glow of distant star
The sun's warm rays that beam from far,
Th' Autumnal kiss of gentle Dew
That glisters light on petal's hue,
The leaf that earthward twists and twirls
With eddying breath of zephyrous swirls
In all of these, my love, thou art
Yet, deep, thy rest is in my heart.

Joseph Fairhurst

Cutting The Ties That Bind

I stood in the centre of the room
Looking at the letters I had written to you
Lying on the floor like autumn leaves
Cast down by a cold north wind
You had brought them back to show me
As if I could not remember writing them
The pages of our relationship
Strewn like rose petals after the storm
I stooped to pick them up
To try and make some kind of order
Out of the chaos and realised then
That I had been doing this with our lives for some time
The futility of it all was evident
To all who cared to look I just never had
You looked at me then and I knew that all was lost
I can never see things as they really are
Until they are staring me in the face
I guess that's just the way I am
Too late to change now you said
We have simply grown apart you added
I just didn't understand your needs you finished
There was nothing simple about it from where I was standing
Surrounded by the wreckage of our life together
I remember other times when things were different
Choosing to remember the good rather than the bad
Has become a habit of mine it seems
After you had left kissing me on the cheek like an old friend
I stood looking out of the window at you
Striding down the road with your shoulders back
Best foot forwards marching into your future
The one without me in it
Even then I could not help but wish you well
After all you are still my daughter
And nothing can change that.

Michael Green

NAKED

I've stripped these lines bare like faces that passed me by
Where I saw through the concealment of the outside.
I've put my lines to the test of real investment
And here my heart sits naked like body flesh.
I know my ink lacked intimacy initially embedded with hardship literacy
And now naked words stripped to the shaped figure of me.
It's this page of pages, memoirs in stages of statue form and phrases
Simply naked like nobody,
No skin that rips as deep as the bleeding of this ink that defines the distinct interlink of me stripped naked
Here with you we fit unconcealed inside my naked mind
Where no clothes cover front or behind just a face fate place and solidified.
There is no escape just the wanting to retrace and invade through our every vein,
This naked love was never blind never covered never denied
Never disguised never defied non devised,
Through every chastise of our lives now only stripped we comply.
Where love dripped, tears slip thick whipped and outstripped,
Of love that rips with hand grips and reveals you in me naked.
Where feelings manifest and out caress a love fest contest,
This naked express willing to be under your arrest where our memories are sacred, this is love naked.

Nadia Fahmy

A VALENTINE WISH

A Valentine wish
Of a tender loving kiss upon your sweet lips
Makes me tingle all over.
So please wait till the day when I am older
Till we marry I am only 8 so please wait till I am 9
Then I'll make you mine so please be mine
Please hang on
I'll throw a penny in the fountain
To make my Valentine wish.

Deborah Storey

Memories Of The Future

If fortunes are fair, and providence kind,
I wish for the photo album of my mind
To be filled with our stories already told,
And reminiscence of our future yet to unfold.

See you smiling, sea-salt skin, waves riding
Sunset walks, hand in hand, gently guiding
In locations we have yet to discover.
Wondering and exploring with each other.

Evoke memories of music not yet composed.
Laughter and conversations yet to be supposed.
Recapture warmth as beside me you awake
Bed linen crumpled from the love we have yet to make.

Sensations still unrelished, bittersweet tears.
The comfort of sharing our autumnal years.
When clarity recedes, I wish my cinematography to be
Visions of a life lived full, together you and me.

Sigrid Marceau

A Valentine Message

From a rosebud
A red rose grown
Its redness glows

In the garden it stands out from
The rest

Roses stand for the true meaning of love
Love is like a rose

A rose continually grows

A rose is picked from where it grows
Next year that special rose will appear
Love will it continually grow

Like a Valentine only they will know
A rose for ever will grow.

M Groves

The First Hours

The darkness tumbling around me
Confusing, confining, painfully morose
The longing inside stifling me, echoing in my head
'It's over,' tears falling, cascading
Filling the midnight hours and
Stretching far beyond
Further than I dare to think
Please don't let me think beyond
This nightmare, my throat tight and dry
The anguish, suffering, fear and loneliness
How can I go beyond this point!
Unless perhaps once more I see his face
Feel his touch, just one more time, please
Just a glimmer of hope, let it be
Just one more look, a smile
One word to comfort me
And yet I know deep within my heart
That this can never be
Now must I strive to fill my life again,
Treasuring that special moment that we shared
In time a happy memory recalled
Once I have gained my life and not despaired
This hour will fade and soon will pass away
But just at present for this short, sharp while
I am blind, and cannot see my way.

Susie Sullivan

Will You

Will you be my light through my darkest days,
Will you be my shelter through the pouring rain.
Will you be my steps when times are low,
Will you be my rope until I let go.
Will you be my guidance when all else is lost,
Will you be my bridge when life gets too hard to cross.
Will you be my strength when I've given up on hope,
Will you be my life and never let me go?

Nadine Smart

Cold Love

I should have sensed the subtle change in you,
Seen through the veil of love's deception.
I had no warning of your changed affection
And thought our new-found love was strong and true.

Sleepless in the longest night of winter,
In mind-numbing cold, frozen to the bone,
I lie between the chill white sheets alone.
Bright between the curtains shines a splinter
Of silver moonlight, gleaming like a sword.
Even if you had pierced me with cold steel
The death of love could not have been more real
But you just spoke those cruel, killing words.

You said, in such a cool, determined voice
'I'm leaving you, I really have no choice.'

Gillian Saunders

Happy Nations Have No History

Loves not lived out are happiest,
My dear and present Love – savour then
This short, unseasonable spring and dark
Will never be quite dark again.

We have no future and no past:
Barren our embrace – yet how we hold
Tight to what means so little and so much:
Never such a love, leaving no trace nor scar.

Recollection will not wrinkle up our love,
Nor wear it out with weight of years.
But when age has conquered lust and I become
A memory whose name you fumble to recall.

Yet will some few faint scraps of music
Echo still and sigh and you will smile
And feel again the sweetness flow around
Your heart and kindle in your eyes.

Jill Truman

SEVEN YEARS (IF EVER YOU SHOULD LEAVE ME)

Not for a second do you leave my thoughts
For just as you promised me you would stay with me
Our whole lives long
So do I want
No – need – a lifetime and beyond
I do not want to see the planes of your face
Changing from a young man's face
I do not want your hair to stop
Its youthful springing through my fingers
I do not want it to come to this
This sudden, sad, bitter truth that scornfully lingers
Seven years we have always had between us, you and I
But, in my thoughtlessness, I considered it nothing at all
Now, suddenly it seems to me nightly that I hear
The Owl's unbidden, omened call
And know that those seven years
Have condensed not into days
Nor hours, nor even minutes
But to shifting seconds
That fall, and fall again
As stinging cold as a winter rain
Seven years was nothing I thought
But know now it is such a little time
But surely not ever time spent in vain.

Sheila Sharpe

Lost Love

A hundred years ago or so
There would have been written proof
Of my love for you and yours for me.
Neatly written words with flamboyant loops
Wrapped around my hopes for the future.
Letters lovingly folded and refolded after
Being read and re-read for reassurance.
Carefully replaced in fragrant envelopes
Kept safe, secure from the loveless world.
The years of our romance bound
In lavender ribbon securing our past together
And as time sped by and hopes faded
To be read, in an amber Autumn afternoon
Through watery blue eyes, for one last time.
So that I could relive the love
Of a lifetime, not with regret
But with gratitude that once,
If only for a brief while,
I was truly loved by you.
But today all I have is vague memories
Of scattered telephone calls which
Once made are forever lost.
No mementos for old age, nor soft phrases
To prompt the failing memory,
Only the empty sound of a telephone
That no longer rings with
Love from you to me.

Sue Gerrard

When I Am Gone
(Dedicated to my wife, Sheila, to my daughter, Labhan and my sons Gaelan, Canice and Saoirse)

When I am gone
Feel me in the life
Around you.

In the kiss of the sun
The touch of the rain
The push of the wind

When snow falls
I am there

Hear me
In the crunch of frost
The cry of a child
The call of the birds . . .

Yes, when I am gone from your sight
Know that I am with you always.

Liam Ó Comáin

My Love

Soft was his voice,
Like the silken shawl,
Tender was his heart,
And heartbeat of,
Loveable rhythm,.
Bravest from the brave,
Was his fury.
Unbeatable,
His talent of vocal love ballads,
'Stole her heart,
The speech of every maiden,
Was he,
My heartbeat;
My only love . . .

Jigna Patel

ACHLUOPHOBIA

Might I get love if you pour sand into this heart?
With my public hands tear your private Hell apart?
Dreams till so ripped open, my tears emerge as fangs,
Thinking of her hangman's noose, where my tattered soul still hangs,
Weeping now, it suffocates, each breath not meant to be,
Yet how can I be a prisoner, when my thoughts are still so free?
How is it you see me, when I cannot find myself?
Why is it that my bleeding heart lies naked on the shelf?
Awakened from reality, to walk again in dreams,
Raped again by whispers, the foreboding of my screams.#
I liked you so for saving me, and loved you still for not,
Worshipped you for building me a Hell, a grave, a cot.
Wrapped so sound in words I never meant to say,
In love with the idea of you, the director, not the way.
A side of you I never knew, laid so for all the rest,
Memories of the future, just seem to me a test,
Of how far this road will take me, how deep this river runs,
Russian Roulette with broken hearts in one barrel of two guns.
And yet if sand you give me, my wounds might now be true,
Till then these public hands will hold each vein so tight,
Safe inside your private Hell, your papier mâchê night.
This line to you, my love, I wrote before I forgot:
I love therefore I am. But when I am, I'm not.

Chris Glover

Purity Of Forever

Amidst mountain dew of our feelings desire, in the flowing rapids of its liquid fire,
Juxtaposed thoughts of fight or flight reveal a life where you stay the night.
Forever within your karmic dress, weaved for a moment beyond this mess;
We step beyond the right and wrong, for above it sounds our familiar song.

Life too small to hold us down, too large is the strength of love renowned.
A sword and shield with which we fight the falser truths from a black mutt's bite.
They tell us this and they tell us that as their pack of lies grow ever fat,
But seeing through their rolling fog is a beginning's hope in slaying dog.

Hand in mine, like anvil in vice as solid grip that they cannot sacrifice,
Upon alter of their own lost sense as we strive to bring them recompense.
The path we walk in need of selves cuts through the dark and deeper delves;
Committing in its tearing wake to refix the quilt that past did make.

At last the dawn can bring us lights from which each other's heart ignites.
The world will find its meanings fought, in lesson love that our souls have taught.
Example to all and not sin within closet, the truth of forever's our next life's deposit;
To spin our dance with a perfect placed step from divine adoration we gladly accept.

Nathan Rowark

The First Adventure

That shadowy entrance, subdued glint, spark of eyes!
You trod all cultures with your classic grace
Of posture, figure, profile

The breathy touch, so tentative,
The answering squeeze

All beams and tiptoes as we trod
Unspoken message:
'The dream's come true'

The curtain nearly volunteered
To close itself.

I was poised to give the word;
Fired by our kisses, you took it from my mouth

Each garment spoke surrender as it fell
A flower-show of fabrics
Adoring those limbs which they had covered;
Warm air on new divested skin
Near liquid in its heady density

Our bodies new-revealed, dreamed up
A gallery of art-figures,
Our mounting breath
Kindled their animation in our honour

Those facing entities suffused with mutual nourishment
The rising sun the backcloth of our dual climax
The bathing epilogue
The farewell walk
A froth of blossom round our tender steps

That fleeting perfection was the purest art
Framed in an idyllic memory.

David Russell

Hidden Desires

Beneath cool surfaces,
Hidden desires flicker and smoulder
Like hesitant fires.
With eye to eye contact, a heart skips a beat.
It's more than pure chance that their glances should meet.

Through echoes of promises never to stray,
Comes a woeful sigh, and a tear brushed away.
But a kiss between spirits forbidden to touch
Dispels the resolve, which they'd heeded so much,
To stay pure in body if not in mind,
And they yield to the passion, now instant and blind.

They hold and they kiss, and they whisper and cry
In submission to love that refused to die.
Yet, they know in their hearts
That whatever transpires
They must break
And have only their Hidden Desires.

Bill Eden

Angel

I've been around for many years, had relationships many with tears,
The darkest thoughts the deepest pain, was too much to cope with too much to strain
I often thought that I should give up on love until I saw an angel from above
She showed me what I had become, and from all love I would always run
She took my hand and made me see, what a broken heart was doing to me
She touched my head and made me see, a beautiful woman, a new love for me
Who was this woman I did not know but on my travels I should go
She wiped my tears and said goodbye, floating up into the sky
I walked the Earth days, weeks and years, looking for the woman I saw in my tears
I gave up hope and felt blue, then came the day when I saw you
I remembered your face from years ago, what should I say? I do not know?
We shared a glance a smile too, from that day on I never felt blue
When I leave I leave my heart with you, and once again I start to feel blue
When I was alone, when I felt blue, that wasn't the first time when I saw you
Because when I was alone and feeling so blue, the angel that came that angel was you.

Gordon Bruce

A Plea To Saint Valentine

Dear Saint Valentine, this day of yours
Seems to have been made for blushing youth,
For those who stand tiptoe on the brink of life,
Still firm and beautiful. But what, we ask,
About the woman whose children have flown the nest,
Loves the world, still feels young but sidelined,
Like an invisible wallflower at a cosmic party,
Petals fading but dying to be asked to dance?
You will see us, if you really look, hovering around
The stands of roses, looking down at their faces,
Their velvet ephemeral faces, their glorious deep reds,
Wondering if we should buy our own, relegated
As we are to housekeepers, to rememberers of birthdays,
To food stockers and menu makers. I pause with a woman,
An unknown woman with a pleasant face, and we smile,
And she says, with a catch in her voice, that she is planning
To buy roses for the grave of her son now in Heaven,
And my eyes gleam tears for her. I murmur in sympathy,
My loneliness suddenly trivial. So dear Saint Val,
Blessed saint, find us all a dream love with the biceps of Rafa,
The lips and sulky presence of Brad or Jude, the charm of George,
A heavenly voice like Josh to serenade us on a sea-swept beach,
And above all the humour to make us laugh out loud.
We will wake on the morrow to find that we are still alive
With passion, rumpled and flushed, strewn with petals,
Rubenesquely dimpled and sprawled, rosily wreathed in smiles,
And with a long lost feeling of having been truly loved.

Liz Davies

ANNIVERSARY

Aloft, on some craggy tor we sat
And peeked at the district over duffled collars;
Smitten by the bracing air that blew;
Cleft in two, but close

Before us, green fields rose into blunted peaks
And fell into gentle dales
Like some heavy swell of an ocean of earth

Above, an English heaven pregnant with rain
Umbrella'd the twain of us;
And around bovine, equine and sheepish behaviour
Farmed itself out as of a patchwork of nature's fabric

And I don't think those feet in ancient time walked up on England's mountain's green
But I believe if we had looked without our London eyes we might have seen
Him, the eternal pariah
The shepherd messiah
In every layer of joy and just impediment
The months and years of silt and sediment
Built up of all we gain and lack.
My prayer is that he will carry us on his back.

At last, we wandered downward
From our vantage hand in hand
As my touch has wandered o'er her skin
Like some green and pleasant land

And as I did look at every nook and crease
Of her windswept face
I thought there is no better place
I would rather be
Happy happy happy
Anniversary.

Peter Thomas

A Taste Of Love

I hunger for a taste of love
But find the cupboard bare,
I lick my lips for lingering crumbs
But love has none to spare.

Fill me up with sweet emotion
Ease the rumblings of my heart,
Fatten me with pure devotion;
Let pastry arms encrust my tart.

Clog my veins with sultry sighs
And ice my cake with kisses;
Don't poison me with covert lies
Or flavourless dismisses.

Though starving now, I do admit –
I've tasted love before;
In gluttony I gorged on it
Till I was sick and sore.

The secret truth of food and love
Is found in moderation,
Excess is reminiscent of
The painful deprivation.

So take love with a pinch of salt
And switch to low-fat cream,
A healthy, balanced heart exalts
In love's delicious dream.

Billie Dee Gianfrancesco

God Is Love

God is love
And love is God
Listen to your heart
And follow the truth
This world is full of traps
And beware of awful sin

Let love in
And let it bloom
There is love waiting
For you in the best
Places and in faces
Who shine bright

This winter is nearly over
And make a new start
Chase the blues away
And love and respect
Yourself more
Your destiny is unfolding
Walk through that door

God is love
And trust and obey
Use all your talents
And sparkle and shine
Give a helping hand
To people in need

Be sure and think
About what you say
Stop, wait and go
Into love, love, love.

Kenneth Mood

21 Grams

I look at you
But look on the inside of you.
Inside your skin.

So I see, what you are
Not just the smiling outside
That comes to the world
I see much more
In
You.

Not the heart
But the goodness of the heart
The laughter
That fills the air around you.
Where it comes from.

They say that when everybody dies
They lose 21 grams.

That is what I search for in you
But in the live body
And I find it
Every
Day.

Marc Carver

BOXES

If you tip me
my tears will spill to the floor
like diamonds.

The most valuable thing
I own and they're yours
as you leave.

I call for others, my mother's words
like a crutch
to hold me up.

Or down as it turns out.
She says
you're taking the things

We collected and made
our whole existence is leaving
in boxes marked

'Fragile – lift with care'.
A week passes
and I come back to our home,

to our bed.
I stand in the kitchen and scream
your name

collapse to my knees
as I find
that you're not there.

Natalie Rogers

ON THE RAILWAY BRIDGE

Misty peach hills
Low sun and pale skies,
An aquatic light
Restrained; northern,
A slight chill
In the tender air.

No birdsong or rush of wind,
Stillness, a trickling brown stream,
Rough dead grass
And you – standing
Willowy and pale
On the bridge.

A fog, dense and grey
Has hidden the misty hills
Shrouded the low blank fields
And hedgerows edges,
Touched your hair
And caressed your sad smile.

Then you are gone.

Leigh Jones

THINKING OF YOU

Golden palomino
How you raced,
Head held high.
Neck to neck,
Reined gripped.
Your hooves cut the ground
In a galloped embrace.
Your breasts are moist in sweat
Waves crash on waves
Night billows in sheets
Twisted, turns, gasps salted breaths,
Stride upon stride,
Stretch after stretch,
It beats. Your saddled,
Sweltered flanks are wet with brine.

John Greeves

OUR HEARTS WILL BEAT AS ONE

The unconditional love we share
Will never fall foul to pain.
Our tears of infinite joy
Will wash away the rain.

I will always love you darling –
No matter where you are.
Our love will shine much stronger
Than the brightest star.

Morning, noon and night,
My thoughts are filled with you.
And the love I feel inside my heart
Will always be so true.

My heart will know no fear
So long as you are with me.
Together our hearts will beat as one
And our love will last for eternity.

Peter Steele

LOVE'S LONE ROSE

A hazy miasma is gathering within my mind,
Echoing memories of our love's bygone times,
As we walked hand in hand, through fields of rich clover,
With the buttercups' bright rays reflected in your smile,
But the sorrow of my days, whelming in your eyes,

Weep not, weep not . . . for my passing of bloom,
As the blossoms in life, doth fade away too soon,
Yet you brightened my days as the birth of a rose,
With the breath of an angel, soothing my soul,
Your radiance within still a passion to behold,

As my being now flows into Forget-me-Not days,
The reminiscences of our love, shall not be allayed,
Forever lingering, as of bird's rapturous song in your heart . . .
Thus the memories passed into the immortality of time,
Shall be there as solace, for my Love's Lone Rose . . .

Barry Pankhurst

PYRENE

Where on earth do you lie, lovely Pyrene
Is it under the snow capped heights?
For there you fled.
Do you now haunt those rocky spurs
On moonlit nights
To keep a ghostly sojourn
With godlike Hercules?
He who scorned the wrath
Of your father King Berbrynx
Whom he failed to please,
For you were savaged by a bear
When Hercules' help you sought
It's said you sometimes a midnight traveller tease
Floating through the stately trees
In the hills that bear your name,
The awesome Pyrenees.
Here your fabled treasure lies,
Crysau crystal and the pearls
In the famous Lebriver caves,
And so the legend lives on of you.

Colin Burnell

Phillip's Pleasure

Phillip's life has been topped
By a note he received
In Thursday's e-mail crop;
Are eyes being deceived?

A stranger fantastic
From distant foreign parts,
Quite enthusiastic
He says, in 'Heart to Hearts'.

To him it's a poser
Of how they'll share their time
If they get much closer
Young love's feelings sublime.

They've met twice you see
Down at seafront shelter,
Watching the azure sea,
Eyeing 'Helter-Skelter'.

He read the note aloud,
Which ended LOL.
Lots Of love? Laugh Out Loud?
It's time to take a stroll.

David Youlden

TWO SOULS
(For Vicki)

We love to race where angels fear to tread
We do this on impulse with no feelings or dread
Walk on fire with the heat under our feet
It's with this impulsion two souls get to meet.

In the night hours when all shadows enrapture
It is in this moment that we always capture
Our deepest and most secret deadly desires
We stay conscious until the moon expires.

Multi-faceted souls on the edge of a precipice
Don't pray for something when we can gladly wish
For the deep innermost levels of the human psyche
Forever looking for the peace and the harmony.

And beware of these dark days or nights
As we hide our feelings behind hidden doubts
All we question in this the human existence
Is the failings of others and their lost resistance.

Dramas, disillusionment or broken hearts
Will not ever enter at the end or the start
We express the diverse sides of the personality
And forever stay in the safety of our sanctuary.

Steven Michael Pape

VALENTINE

Look at my face
What do you see?
It's cracked with life,
Time's gift to me.

My teeth are unpearly,
My hair's worn quite rough,
Unruly's the body,
Feet corned and tough.

And what of my spirit?
It's strong and it's true.
We've had many crisis
But I'm still here with you.

Sally Plumb

LOVE AND OTHER VALUES

How do we cheat banality
And this sitcom dialogue?

How do we stay in love
Without any subject matter
While we fix tyres and taps?

I thought without thinking
I'd be entertained by now
By something like genius

I felt without any feeling
I'd have somebody else
To tease and resurrect
In the likeness of loving

You imagined that work
Would keep you slim –
That you'd be significant
Without raising children

I thought I would be gone

How do we love each other
When there's always daylight
Emptying a fetid bedroom
Of romance and pleasure

You have never worn
A full-length mink coat
To watch the dawn arrive

I will always want rest
While you flatter the chorus
And men in cummerbunds

I say love is a silence

You say love is a fast car

Robin Lindsay Wilson

Fifty Years On

Fifty years ago
You knelt down and asked me
To marry you. I was surprised, but
I just said 'Yes.' And we kissed,
As in the best romantic film.
Yet we were not very 'romantic' . . .
We came from different countries,
Spoke different languages, but
We looked towards the same horizon.

We met at a university dinner
In a venerable English city,
We smiled and you said,
'Come and sit next to me.'
As I started a darkish broth
You whispered in my ear
'I can cook better than that!'
You were a don who could
Make me laugh! I felt happy.

Later on we could agree on politics:
You hated extremists, this made me rejoice.
You were a free-thinker, a true soulmate for me!
You loved France, my country.
Its literature, its art, its music, its food,
Of course, the family cats I told you about.
You wanted the world happier, not richer.
And then I knew we were
Genuinely in love.

Together we created a home,
Supporting each other in a new world..
Children, then grandchildren were born.
We shared thrills, joys, pain, grief,
Our love helped us survive,
Traumatic loss: our first born.
Our beloved beautiful daughter
Snatched away by cancer.
She lives on within both of us.

In the last phase of our life
We still love each other,
Always shall. I know
You can't kneel any longer
But we can still hold hands.
Fifty years later you still say
'Come and sit next to me.'

Antoinette Marshall

Lost Love

They told me it was for the best,
In marriage I would find no rest.
They spoke of more fish in the sea,
That he's not good enough for me.

They said I could build a new life,
But without him it's like a knife
Cutting up my heart to the quick,
Deeper, ever deeper, each nick.

No one said how to stop the pain,
The mem'ries that come yet again.
Instead the tears come like rain,
Running down a cold windowpane.

The light has gone, I'm dark and still,
A big black hole I cannot fill.
They don't see I'm an empty shell,
Living a life that is a hell.

Gwendoline Douglas

GATES CLOSED

My world is looking down the drive,
Budding trees keep me alive,
Brave beauties stare before they bloom,
Spring daffodils will be out soon.

Along the ancient wooden fence
Climbing plants flowers dispense,
Black cat slinks by with dab of paw,
Her sultry glide my eyes adore.

There is another world outside
But that's beyond where I abide,
It seems so fast with flowing cars
I'd rather gaze at silent stars.

Full moon in crisp and coldish sky
With Venus bright and moons nearby,
Groups of sparkle through the night,
Space clouds drift, pure wondrous sight.

So deep go feelings for my scene,
For this is me, my whole, my mean,
My touch and stroke is done by eye,
Such love is mine but my heart cries.

Poor plan is done to make me safe,
Keep out the hoods, the nettle waif,
My world, my slender track just froze,
Cold shuttered gates have now been closed.

Nick Clifton

The White Sports Car

He jumped nimbly into the white sports car
Revved the engine and swung into the road
Hood back and hair ruffled by the wind
The car was soon out of sight and earshot.
A brief encounter – so soon gone forever.
My heart stopped in its tracks.

So suddenly it flashed upon my mind
That other time, that other place long ago
That other white sports car, that other face.
The fair hair, the smiling, wrinkled blue eyes Which made my poor heart overflow with love,
With an undying passion.

I would watch every morning from the window
Straining my ears for sounds of its approach
Desperate for his smile and cheery wave,
Watching the car disappear round the bend.
Knowing that we would meet later that day
To talk and laugh again.

That wonderful day he took me for a ride.
Sitting beside him – just the two of us.
The sun on our backs and wind in our faces.
Happy, carefree, living in the moment,
As if we were the only two people on earth
Living the dream of love.

I wanted it to last for a lifetime
But our paths were destined never to join
Diverging to distant parts of the world.
My heart never forgets the passion and the dream
Of all that could have been – another life,
Riding the white sports car.

June Smith

First Born

You were our First Born, content, forever smiling,
With cornflower blue eyes that were so beguiling,
At the age of eighteen months, and heart stoppingly bonny,
You took your first steps for your devoted Granny.
Then three years later when you started infant school,
You were quiet and shy and wore a smile that never cooled,
Dear Little daughter.

At seven you enjoyed Brownies, but never took to Girl Guiding,
Then worried Dad and me when you took up horse riding.
Two years later, as school homework started growing
Gymkhanas with Dabby were thankfully slowing.
Moving brought new friends and soon you were dreaming,
Teenage dreams as The Osmonds had you all screaming,
Dear Teenage Daughter.

At fifteen it was Youth Club, Pop Concerts, roller skating,
Blue eyed and pretty, before long you were dating.
Today, a High Flyer, chockfull of 'expertise',
You juggle wife, mother, daughter roles with amazing ease.
So many happy memories, there's just one thing to say,
You were loved – and still are – from that very first day,
Dear Grown-up Daughter.

Betty Lightfoot

A Fleeting Meeting

This is a secret,
Up till now, that I have kept.
Last night I went to sleep
And while I slept
I was transported
And my spirit leapt.

How could it happen?
However could this be?
For there you were
In Paradise with me.

We wandered in a meadow
Near a stream
I pinched myself and asked
'Is this a dream?'

But no! – we splashed barefoot
I felt the water, cool
Then hugged you
As we rested by a pool.

I smelled your perfume -
You were really there
You smiled and ran your fingers
Through my hair.

And just as joy transcended –
It ended . . .
I woke with feelings
That I can't explain.
Perhaps tomorrow night
We'll meet again.

Jonathan Bryant

Where Does Love Come From?

Where does love come from? Where does it start?
Does it come from the head? Does it come from the heart?
Is it seen with our eyes? Is it felt in our arms?
Is it something we earn? Is it found in a charm?

Is love a beginning, or is it an end?
Is it seen in the smile or the hug of a friend?
Does love begin on a wedding day?
Is it here for a lifetime? Is it here to stay?

Does it come when a baby arrives on the scene?
Is it captured in a rainbow, or a mountain stream?
Is it found in the dew of a springtime morn?
Or in a snowflake, on a cold, crispy dawn?

But wait, right at the beginning, before time began,
God's love was there, and it stretches life's span.
This was love's beginning, this was its birth.
God's love came to man when Jesus came to Earth.

This was love at its purest, this was love at its best.
It's the love that goes on loving, when put to the test.
It's the love that forgives, it's the love that paid the price.
It's the love that Jesus showed in His final sacrifice.

I can now love my neighbour, God's love can flow through me.
I am loved, I can go on loving, because this love is free.
God's love does have a beginning, but it has no end.
There's no other love like it, and it's ours, my friend.

God loves us, and we are so precious to Him,
His love, comes to heal, and restore us within.
Let's turn to Him now, take hold of His hand,
And together with love, we'll reach out to this land.

Pauline Hamilton

PRECIOUS LOVE

Love so precious, love so true,
Is the love I have for you.
My heart is yours, and all that I own,
Since knowing you, my love has grown.

Your face so dear to me,
Is all I ever need to see,
When darkness threatens every day,
Seeing you, it clears away.

Your smile, your laugh, brings out the sun,
Scatters the clouds like so much dust.
How could I not love you
Nothing to me could mean as much
As your nearness, your loving touch.

To feel your love, your kisses sweet,
So close I feel your beating heart,
It beats with mine, we are as one,
My love, I know we'll never part,
Our souls belong together,
And will always be, when life is done,
For our love will last forever.

Grace Maycock

Over June Lane

Miranda,
As you move between the rocks,
Gold as the sun your uncut locks,
And turn in its light,
The long night coming from over the sky,
O I never, in all my days,
Knew a gaze that rivalled yours,

No, I never,
Though I went so far,
Met the girl that you are
In any teeming town,

Miranda,
You and I in a tiny shop,
On a corner in a street when England was sunny,
And the morning late,
And free from the gate of a child-filled school
You waited that I take you hand-led to the hill;

Only you, Miranda,
And a setting of the sun,
Only you by the shadowy rock
You lay your hand upon,
The water twisting in the wood,
The high dark waiting to come,
When you dreamed in the grass and your voice was mute
And all the safe daylight gone,

Only you, Miranda,
And a wordless voice of love,
On leaves above a heedless town,
Ever golder your hair
In a high moon lifting;

Only you, Miranda,
And a dusk upon the hill,
And what I say in certain suns,
On fields a long-gone girl had run in,
Is like a longing for a morning,
Gardens wet we met and ran in,
With the see-through river ringing
In the dark of a silent wood.

Kevin Ryan

LONGING

Off to visit my loved one I am soon to go
But oh my does not the waiting time go slow?
Why is it that for good times one must wait?
I always try to be early and not late for this date
She knows that my heart belongs to her and her alone
We fill in the waiting time by talking on the phone
I know it sounds as though I am wishing my life away
But I want to be with my precious one every day
Waiting and longing to be together gives me a great pain
For my darling I desperately want to be with her again
I count the days and then the hours that I know
Will drag by slowly until it's time for me to go
When I arrive there will be many tears of delight
For I will hold her and hug her with all my might
We will then be together so close not wanting to part
For she is my Sweetheart and I love her with all my heart.

Leonard A G Butler

MY LOVE

My love is like a fresh spring day
That graces an April morn
So sweet and fragile as a rose
Without a single thorn

My love is like a summer's day
Drowned in honeysuckle and thyme
Their fragrant perfumes fill the air
As I hold your hand in mine

My love is like an autumn day
In tones of gold and brown
With leaves fanned by a bustling breeze
That gently blows them down

My love is like a winter's day
Sparkling snowflakes drifting by
Falling to their destiny
Just as you and I.

Susan Jacqueline Roberts

To My Wife On Our Golden Anniversary

And on our magic wedding day
Those fifty years ago
We couldn't know the future
How were we just to know

We joined in love together
Our course was roughly set
We sailed through life these fifty years
And we are sailing yet

We built our home and family
As partners shared a life
Our love cloaked gently round us
Children, man and wife

Of course we had the problem times
When life was not too smooth
But we survived those problem times
As only love would prove

I thank you for these fifty years
I thank you for my life
I love you and I thank you
That you're my loving wife.

Ray Ryan

The Miscarried Child

You were so small to cross
The River Styx alone with
Charon. How did you pay?
You did not ask me
For the fare . . .
You asked for nothing,
But I began to knit for you
A heart, a small pair of
Lungs, toes, fingers that
Were twined already in my heart.

Rapt in concentrated brooding
We grew together. Child of
My mind, I gave you love and
Patience, but you could not wait.
Had I pinned you more securely
To me, would you have grown –
Perfect?

If you have form or meaning
Now, are you as strong
As courageous as your brother –
My first (my much beloved) son.

Janet Harmer

And These Two Are One!

They two were walking.
Rainbow flowers greeted them.
These two had no haste.
Hawaii's palm trees,
They would move from side to side,
And they were placid.
The sun had gone down.
It was dark on the ocean,
And they had passion.
He caressed Suzanne,
And he touched her with his lips.
She knew he loved her.
They were on the land.
They were close to the water.
It was a blue sky.
Suzanne responded.
She caressed Dennis' lips.
She showed tenderness.
The heavenly moon,
It was pleasing both of them.
They loved the islands.
The sea was so big.
The waves sang a lullaby.
They showed the land love.
Pale purple flowers,
All of them were bending down,
And these two saw them.
Dennis promised her.
He would raise Suzanne's spirits.
He would make her glow.
Suzanne and Dennis,
They were looking at mountains.
Dennis was yearning.
Dennis longed for her.
Suzanne saw this in his eyes,
And she vowed marriage.
Dennis is not sad.
He is not apart from her,
And these two are one!

Laraine Smith

SOULMATES JOURNEY

As I roam on my journey . . . through space and time,
On a sea of music . . . my joy does climb,
And sails through clouds . . . .in floating rhyme,
My endless serenity sways . . . in forests of golden pine.

A mist of peace . . .swirls below and above,
Surrounded by contentment . . . embraced in love,
Against a vision of beauty . . . my ecstatic feelings rub,
And soar around the universe . . . as a heavenly dove.

Starlight candles light . . . my soulmate's path,
A pure white landscape . . . coloured by an angelic laugh,
As the senses blaze . . . stroked by spirit's staff,
We find tranquility . . .soaking in the cosmic bath.

Powdered in aromas of mystic perfume,
Invisible flowers bloom . . . for touch to consume,
Treasures piled high . . . in an infinite room,
Celestial soulmates dine . . . on a harvest moon
Eternity toasts: the bride and groom.

Michael Levy

THOSE FIVE WONDERFUL DAYS

Here I am not feeling well,
There's not much for me to tell.
At the summer school this year,
I met someone very dear.

When I wrote to him last week,
There were some words I couldn't speak,
He meant everything to me,
He was my special friend, you see?

He was so nice; he was so kind,
A friend like him is hard to find,
My heart is truly missing him,
I have to wake up from this dream.

Minerva Pinciu

Roura

You stand before a window but I cannot see your face.
The glass is frozen and so is your breath.
The flakes of snow turn you into lace
And rays of sun melt icy wrath.
But you glitter with pain and glass loses warmth.
The tears rain and rain and candles gutter in chorus.
You gulp in the frosty air and life returns.
Why should we both care that sunset fails?

Roman Mikhalyuk

Maybe That's You . . . !

An adolescent feeling . . .
Reminds me about the kiss I consumed . . .
One twilight evening . . . in my dreams . . .
Invisible to figure out . . .
But it was sweet . . .
In the Garden of Eden . . .
With the aroma of rose . . . and the
Pleasing feathers flying over us . . .
Like a blissful shower of blessings . . .
A zephyr whispering through the trees . . .
As the angels from Heaven . . .
Hum harmonious ballads of Love . . .
I hold back to espy . . . the view . . .
Of the butterflies . . .
Desire to come back to reality . . .
And seek whose amiable emotion . . .
Took me to this paradise . . .
Yet recalling . . .
'Maybe that's you . . . !'

Anne Senanayake

My Honey

My honey
You are always
In my thoughts.

Your tender smile
Is the sunshine
Of my life.

Your faithful love
Is charming fragrance
Of the flowers.

Your pure beauty
Is the vision
Of paradise.

Igor Marinovsky

A Month Before March

Love was madness –
But I welcomed her to my eyes –
So I could solve the puzzle of loss –
Betrayal and heartbreak.

Though I fooled, played around,
She still sent me – Cupid from Jupiter,
To teach me the ways of the love goddess
Cos she was dying – within.

That soulmate is – my February
An anchor to - my ever joy, my story . . .

Michael Kwaku Kesse Somuah

Failure

I never thought I'd meet you
Like a hurricane
You twirled into my life
And caused havoc
In my life . . .
I never thought I'd meet you

My heart bleeds
At the sight of you.
Everything and anything
That would have been,
Could have been,
Should have been,
Is no more, because
I met you.

Like a hurricane you came
And now I'm picking broken pieces of my life
You came in my life unexpectedly
I never thought I'd meet you.

Years and years, seasons and seasons, today came
Yesterday died down in our thoughts.
And never would I have thought of you.
You bring me pain
Embarrassment
Torture.

With stones in my voice I whisper
I never thought I'd meet you
Pensively thinking of now
You remind me of yesterday
Filled with thoughts tasting of seawater.

Kagiso Basetsana Makwatse

In Mother's Lap

In Mother's lap,
A baby finds the world
A world that puts her to sleep of peace and love
And makes all her dreams sweet.

The night dancing
Over the little bay happily,
The wind is passing by
Touching her chubby and sweet cheeks,
And gives her the best kiss
So she won't find any horrible risk,
And all she can have is her sound sleep,

She is not dreaming of a big world,
But a world full of love,
And the mother singing a lullaby
To her
So she won't have any bad thought
In her mind
And she can have not a sleep only
But the good thought
To make her sleep sweeter.

Pushkar Bisht

Love's Eternal Sound

Leap across the mountains
And dance upon the sea.
Sing a song forever
Of mercy that is free.

For Grace has poured sweet Life Divine
Into a dying heart,
And captivating Love surrounds it,
Never to depart.

So let the rivers run with joy
And let the trees resound,
With the superlative anthem
Of Love's eternal sound.

Lisa La Grange

You And Me

Your thoughts are mine
My thoughts are yours
Appearing oft as one

So strange but true
It happens through
Connection of our hearts

We think the same
We feel the same
And hear unspoken words

When love is strong
Our hearts become
Extensions of our hearing

You and me
Becoming one
Through merging of our hearts

We think as one
We feel as one
We live as one forever.

Sarah Zhu

Hidden Love

I am hiding behind the post in your heart,
Are you looking for me?
My love for you is like the restless sea,
Come kiss me again for my heart to be free.
You are the fresh flowers smiling at me,
Your heart is bubbling like the laughing sea.
The sun caressed your face in a thin shower of rain,
Your succulent lips caused my heart to pain.
Your love is hidden in your smiles,
Your innocent face looks like a child.
Your immortal kisses light a lamp in my heart,
In the heat and the cold your love shall never part.
I am hiding in your heart for your love to grow,
Your love comes and goes like the wind that blows.
The rains and the wind called you to me again,
I heard your heart cry for me to feel your pains.
Where are you hiding O my lovely darling?
Come kiss me again in the bright morning!
Let our love grow like the waves in the sea,
For our hearts to rejoice, for our souls to be free.
Your love is hidden in the mirror of your eyes,
Come kiss me again for your love never to die.

Rev Gideon Sampson Cecil

ESSENCE OF LOVE

Sometimes difficult to find,
Sometimes difficult to express,
Sometimes difficult to feel,
But it's there . . . everywhere.

Powerful, cutting as a laser,
Power to wet eyes, melt the coldest of hearts.
To create Heaven . . . hateful love to ruin life.
A cruel weapon oft' wielded foolishly.

Tender as a butterfly's wing . . . gone too soon.
Fragile as morning dew, it commands respect and care
To prevent common guile.
Too long a love-starved world.

Inbred and learnt,
Instinct which needs nurturing,
To receive and give.
For rusty as rust, extremes exist,
Many are guilty and consequences are limitless.

Confusing theologians and simpletons,
From Adam till Apocalpyse,
Its omniscience always felt.
How quickly it is lost and we lament and kill for its return.

Jerome Teelucksingh

Love Is Not . . .

Love is not
Kind nor true,
Blind nor blue,
Breathless nor endless,
Fair nor *doux*.

It is not
All you need,
Sown as a seed,
Nor a banquet on which we feed.

It does not
Make you complete
Nor make your heart beat.

But when love can give and bend, be strong and heal,
Those are the words which make love real.

Michael Seese

Fixed On Red

Somewhere on a thoroughfare bending north
A myriad of thoughts soar in the wind –
Tall in stature, this man of sturdy girth
Fixed on red as wheels spin unconfined.

Stars twinkle in eyes of emerald
As the moon illuminates nocturnal liturgy
He muses metaphors that transcend
Time and space while his language releases energy.

The unseen crown sitting upon his head
Garnets that gleam reflections of belief;
A hidden vestibule of heavens bread
Soothing gloomy hearts downtrodden from grief,

And within his witty helmet covering,
Resides a world of endless discovering.

Carla Iacovetti

Nostalgic Nirvana

Reflecting all around
Rods and cones of my eye
Images of you
Like the stars in the sky

Resonating all around
Cochlea and canals of my ear
Melodies of you
Playing each moment of the year

Gushing ceaselessly
In the tunnels of my nose
Fragrance of you
As a garden full of rose

Flowing endlessly
In the rivulets of my nerves
Your single touch
Fuelling my soul's verves

Carved allover
The museum of my mind
Memories of you
That you left behind

Painted everywhere
On the walls of my heart
Words of yours
Masterpiece of a divine art.

Umesh Rao

MYSTIC CHARM

There's an Irish man
Who comes every night
When my eyes fall shut.
With golden curls and
Sea-green eyes,
He smiles at me with a knowing smile.

I never get to touch him
I never get to feel his touch.
As oceans stand firm between us
But still my heart fills up with love
As with eyes, green as the sea
He smiles at me with that knowing smile.

Zinzile Mngomezulu

WATERFALL OF LOVE

Here
There are no veils of deceit
love defines reason
when we are together

The magnificence of your being
is the simplicity within
intoxicating me with warmth

and your love

your love

Carries me down the river
of sweet tears
into faithful arms eternally ~

Shirley Harrison

Therefore, I Love You

How so, my love, presume I not?
How so, my love, lovest thou me not?
How so, my love, assume I so?
How so, my love, do I love thee?

When, my love, was there ever a peasant
Offering a rose to a king?
Therefore, I presume not

When, my love hast thou looked upon me
With love other than that from a king to a subject?
Therefore, thou lovest me not

When, my love, hast thou not looked upon her
With eyes thirsting for joy?
Therefore, I assume so

Why so, my love
Do the trees bloom in spring
The waters lash the rocks
The wind blow the sailor home?

Why so, my love
Do I love thee?

Nan Collain

Can love be lost

When idle pleasure
Casts its stale perfume
In consciousness' face?
Does a taste endure
Or sound resound
Beyond physicality's embrace?
And yet, amongst this mass
Of senseless sensing,
Of constellation and of space;
Inside the trenchant, grating grind
Of skin and bone, this carbon base
That drips fatality upon decay
And never gives, except itself
In constant attenuated fall . . .
And yet, for all of this,
A touch, a scent, a look,
A memory transforms the sap
Of life into a very siphon
That will draw the amorial source:
A font whose wellspring
Is Eternity itself.

Adrian Pickett

A Savage Heart

Why does a sad heart lock away its feelings?
Why is it so savage?
Why does a sad heart lack the art to express?

Why does a sad heart never cry?
Why does it love no one again?
Why does it isolate itself
And live a life in bane?
Why is it so savage?
Why does a sad heart lack the art to express?

Why does a sad heart not sing in the shower?
Why does it take over the mind?
It searches in the corners of its rooms
For a dream it cannot find.
Why is it so savage?
Why does a sad heart lack the art to express?

Why does a sad heart stay in pain
And live like a pearl in a nutshell?
Why does it wander in vain
Waiting to be soothed by love
That was lost and never found again?
Why is it so savage?
Why does a sad heart lack the art to express?

It speaks never of its scars
Those that,
Cut deep neat with a knife so sharp
It would tear a mountain and its skin of snow apart.
Why is it so savage.
Why does a sad heart lack the art to express?

While incapable to care for itself
It understands the ones in despair
Why does a sad heart not speak yet tell a tale
Not speaking a single word,
It makes the eyes rain?
Why does a sad heart be so savage
Yet write poetry
And lack the art to express?

Nikita Biswal

Nakesendo, Hime No Kaido

Dry morning cold
Snow piling up silently
Houses curving slowly
Along the winding road
Sekigahara cedars watch
A lonely crow
Against the clip-clop
Of a bent figure
Climbing the stone steps
Of Amaterasu shrine.

History is all there
But apart from birds
Only imagination traverses
Real and symbolic distances,
The palanquin trudges
Along the darkening highway
With princess Kazunomiya,
Snaking their way towards Edo
To marry the shogun
In a world-renouncing gesture.

The horses whinny,
The soldiers wheeze,
The villages cumulate their fires
Fixing sake, fish and rice,
And the paper doors flutter
Their translucent pages
Of memory while
The children eager-eyed
Peep inside
Oblivious of any mischance.

At Lake Biwa a last look back
Towards Kyoto,
Of what is left behind in departures
And then the floating world
Moves once more, slowly
Past Sukego villages
Into the modern concerns
Of daily life,
Priorities intrigues,
Profit and loss.

Mukesh Williams

Two Hands

Sitting alone with time to ponder
On World War Two, so long ago,
Scared witless by Britain's blackout,
Not one light allowed to show.
Walking home in that dreaded dark,
A father-figure held my hand
And childhood fears abated.

More time passed. Emotions elated,
My husband's hand I held.
Through many years we've travelled thus,
His strength and comfort undispelled.

Soon I held my toddler's hand
As he learned to walk and run.
Oh happy days of mothering,
With smiles and cuddles and fun.

He's now grown up, caring and kind.
A better son I could never find.
We came upon a busy road
When walking out one day.
Taking my hand he escorted me over
And we were on our way.

Dinah van der Werf

Desire Not Thou Anyone

Desire not thou anyone
For they desire someone, say
The essence is to be great
Thou art can't be so drained.
Once brisk way pave the seed
The weary bed of sand may drag
Though one should lay bare
None can think nor desire
The flare of attraction swipes
Which results in feelings wipe
Melts in the flare rapidly
And makes the yearning go wide.
I knew, and knew well, I can know thee.
The breeze made thee reconcile in me.
No storm, no flood separate anymore,
I see, feel and find thee everywhere
Desire is a squander for many, not me!
I desired and deserve more dearly,
Cherished are you forever heartily,
Dividing thee, I am not what I am,
And be not what I can be.
'Without' is a farfetched image,
Hardly to be drawn a cliché
Once and last to say is just
Cherished are you forever heartily.

Anila Pillai

BENCH, STREET AND WALK . . .

Thinking all the nice times, I had in my life
Tears drop away on my smile
I am not sad, but it's bad
That all good times ended up so early
The bench on which we sat and chat
You come close to me when I stayed back
Your desire, to take me in your arms
And the pain you move away

My bench, street and walk
Want to forget that but I can't
I want to ask you, how to . . .
Let it go.

You placed your head in my lap
I am running my fingers through your hair
You saying to me, not to stop that
And I am watching you, how you close your eyes
Our street of love, we had a lot
While walking you pull me towards you
And when I kiss you
Darkness of that street just move away

My bench, street and walk
I want to let that go but I can't
I wanted to ask you, if you want to
Forget that too

My bench, street and walk
I want to forget that, but I can't
Want to find the way
Want to get away
From whatever I had

Want to be alone
Not to miss anyone
Sweetheart, but tell me the way
Or else I'll be mad
I want to let all go

My bench, street and walk.

Zoha Khalid

DOORS

The smallest second
A weak moment
A rainy rooftop
Time had stopped

Stumbling words
Intoxicated minds
A driven heart
An anxious soul

It touched me
Something heavenly
Something soft
Something sweet

A hallucination
Mere imagination
This delusion
My dilution

Standing stupefied
Completely satisfied
The presence before me had vanished
The thought in me was banished

It touched me
Something heavenly
Something soft
Something sweet . . . pressing against my lips.

Tersia De Jager

Love In Those Days

Love was not so easy those days.
The year had only two months,
December and May
When the vacation brought on his shoulders
Some rare chances of meeting.
The schedule of the spring was different then,
Days were the marks counted daily on the walls,
Nights passed uncounted looking at the stars,
The heart stayed in eyes
And eyes stayed on unending roads.
Angels did visit in disguise of letters and
Secretly resided in the sweaty ravine
Between two small hills.
His only ambassador, the handkerchief
Was the only solace.
Spread his smell around the existence
Whenever unfolded to wipe tears.
The balcony always stood mute
Stretching her eyes
Like the Statue of Liberty,
Always waiting for the arrival
Of her liberator.

Mukeshkumar Raval

ASPECTS OF *Love* - A Collection Of Poetry

Forward Poetry Information

We hope you have enjoyed reading this book - and that you will continue to enjoy it in the coming years.

If you like reading and writing poetry drop us a line, or give us a call, and we'll send you a free information pack.

Alternatively if you would like to order further copies of this book or any of our other titles, then please give us a call or log onto our website at www.forwardpoetry.co.uk

Forward Poetry Information
Remus House
Coltsfoot Drive
Peterborough
PE2 9BF
(01733) 890099